This book is dedicated to my husband and children.
You inspire me to be better every single day!

UN-BREAK IT!
The Simple Way to Improve What's Broken

Jodi Holstein
Explorer of Broken Processes and Architect of Improvement

PROLOGUE

This book was born out of time spent with business professionals, young and old, experienced and novice, management and administrators. Over and over again, these professionals share their frustrations about unmet expectations in their offices, homes, and communities, impacting them personally and professionally. More often than not, these professionals are waiting anxiously for some kind of a solution to make things better. I feel your pain and I know there is help!

The Difference Between
Problem Solving & Process Improvement

As I sat down to complete this book, it was drawn to my attention that I was using the terms "problem solving" and "process improvement" interchangeably. These are not synonymous terms, and maybe this would be a good place for my readers to start.

Process is a fundamental part of every achievement, personal and professional. In every problem encountered, a process failure can usually be found. For instance, "My child won't eat breakfast…" I would ask, "What is your process around breakfast and how could we tweak any of those processes to make the experience better?" Maybe I hear, "My boss doesn't treat me with respect!" My response might be, "What are your processes around communication and how could any of those processes be improved to raise the level of respect?" If I heard, "My event was a flop…" I would question, "What were your processes around marketing and what could be done differently to increase the success?"

With a **problem solving** approach, the goal is generally to completely fix the issue – on the first attempt! This is not a "three strikes" opportunity. You typically get one swing of the bat and the issue must be brought to perfect, resulting in long development times and lots of reviews. More often than not, the goal of "perfectly solved" creates a paralysis of creativity and propels projects into a backward spiral.

The **process improvement** approach, on the other hand, looks for incremental increases over time. Think of it as a continuous effort, not a single event. With process improvement, testing things out, and disposing of attempts that don't work, is encouraged. You're not letting the desire for the perfect solution be a barrier to making something better.

People understand that even the best of the best can get better. Process improvement is an approach that encourages making things better – not perfect.

What? You Don't Have Time?

Good news! This book is short. It's more of a pocket guide because everyone is so busy. Too busy, in fact, to take on one more task or responsibility that will potentially rob us of one more weekend, or one more kids activity, or one more night out with friends. We have a life, and adding more pressure, like having to wade through a book as long as "War and Peace" with no perceivable compensation, will stop us in our tracks.

Process improvement is not a simple or easy protocol. Professionals who have studied and perfected the practice are great assets to their companies; unfortunately, most people don't have the luxury of having those individuals at their fingertips and, therefore, need to do it on their own. This book is written for them!

I believe that while process improvement can be complicated, it can also be boiled down to manageable steps, resulting in the ability to spend time wisely, leaving more time for life.

Who Should Read This!

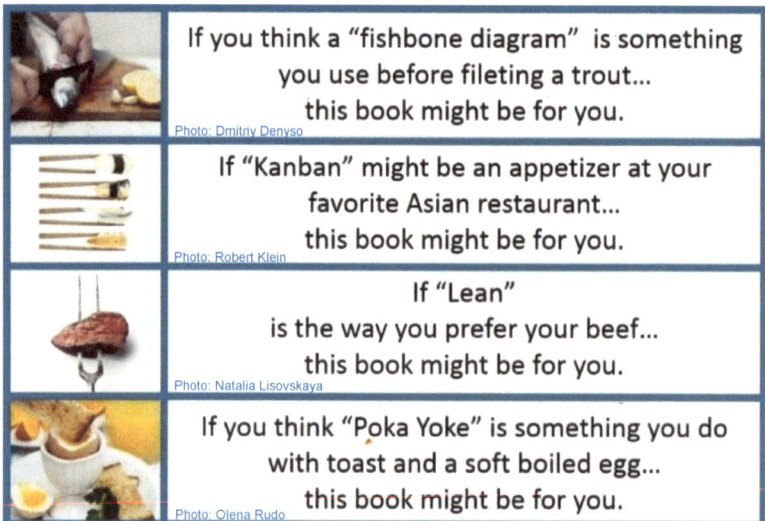

	If you think a "fishbone diagram" is something you use before fileting a trout... this book might be for you. Photo: Dmitriy Denyso
	If "Kanban" might be an appetizer at your favorite Asian restaurant... this book might be for you. Photo: Robert Klein
	If "Lean" is the way you prefer your beef... this book might be for you. Photo: Natalia Lisovskaya
	If you think "Poka Yoke" is something you do with toast and a soft boiled egg... this book might be for you. Photo: Olena Rudo

These, and hundreds of other terms, are common in process improvement circles. Do you have time to learn them?

The information in this book will be valuable to anyone who has had limited exposure to process improvement protocols, but has situations needing improvement. That, my friends, describes the majority of us out there today.

If you could benefit from having a simple, common sense concept in your hip pocket to identify those things that cause you pain, and an easy process for making them better, keep reading! Because, colleges don't include this in most degree programs, employers don't necessarily provide training, and helicopter parents aren't finding it necessary to pass on to their special offspring.

INTRODUCTION

Change is Hard!
Embrace Improvement Instead!

"Even those who fancy themselves the most progressive will fight against other kinds of progress, for each of us is convinced that our way is the best way."
— Louis L'Amour

Change is a word that is thrown around as a mantra or battle cry, always by people who think change is something it's not. The Presidential election of 2008 saw an entire country chanting "change." We need "change." It's time for a "change." The "change" we can trust! I found myself chuckling inside as I heard these phrases over and over. I was amused because all of these people were begging for "change," but that is not really what they wanted.

Does the term change foster thoughts of hope and goodness in you? If your spouse said, "Our marriage has changed," what would your first emotion be?

Photo:
Jessmine

When I said "I wanted to change my look," I didn't expect THIS!!

If your best friend said, "My health has changed," would your initial response be to cheer? Of course not! The truth is that the word change, as much as we say we want it, actually fosters bad feelings.

You see, when someone says, "Things need to change around here!" what they really mean is, "Someone please make things better for me!" The problem is "change" does not mean "make things better." "Change" means to make things different. In the word "different," there is no promise of better. Different can mean frustration to pain, or pain to agony, or productive to inefficient, or healthy to sick, or love to hate, and so on.

I always caution groups who say, "We need to make a change." In my experience, you know you have achieved true change when everyone is equally dissatisfied, and I know that is never the intention of someone crying out for change. Improvement, on the other hand, has the promise of at least moving things in the right direction.

We live in a culture that struggles when it comes to improving painful situations. Taking the 100,000 foot view, how about American politics? *Politifact* reports that Congress has an 11% approval rating, and yet 96% of the incumbents will be re-elected. Clearly we know it's broken, yet we keep voting for the very people responsible. What about Medicare, Medicaid, Disability, and Social Security? Is there anyone in the entire nation that believes these programs are functioning well? I don't think so. Yet meaningful improvements to these programs have failed to yield a true benefit to the people. Why? Because we can't wrap our heads around a total and complete fix, so we surrender.

Coming down a few thousand feet, how about education at the local level? Is society generally happy with students graduating with a 6th grade knowledge of math, the inability to use a pencil, and punctuation that breeds confusion? No! Generally, we want the School Board and Administration to provide a better product. But they don't, and as a culture, we accept that they don't. We are at a loss to understand our personal ability, and dare I say responsibility, to make things better.

It's easy to begin a great job with excitement and vigor, only to become apathetic when the "honeymoon" ends and problems become apparent. We have been conditioned to settle for broken, and as a result have become lazy about exercising our right to create efficiency and effectiveness in every area of our lives, be that our homes, families, communities, businesses, departments, or cubicle spaces.

Exercise is a deliberate word! When we exercise, we must start slow, understand the process and equipment, and grow gradually to expand our capability. Process improvement will need to be an exercise as well, and practice will make us proficient. It takes practice to get great at anything, and being skilled at making things better is no exception.

Being a champion of improvement is not for the faint of heart. Here's what happens when you try to take people from the comfortable and familiar to what is new and unknown... they don't like it! Consider one of two approaches when attempting to get folks thinking and moving in a new direction, the "Hammer" and the "Velvet Hammer."

The Hammer
The "hammer" approach is sometimes necessary when you have a deadline, and quite honestly, your job hinges on the outcome of the improvement. This is the "we don't care how the people feel or how they are impacted" approach, which is not necessarily a team builder. When the team vibe or morale doesn't matter, and only the outcome counts, a hammer is usually the tool of the trade.

With the "hammer" approach, there is little pushback, because the message has been sent (loud and clear) that feedback and/or pushback is not tolerated. This doesn't mean there won't be a lot of negative water cooler talk regarding the new process and the person making that new process happen. It can be unpleasant, and if you are the one wielding the hammer, don't forget that the hammer hurts and people don't always recover well. Business relationships may never be the same.

The Velvet Hammer

Using the "velvet hammer" still prioritizes a successful outcome, but has a much softer approach which considers the impact to the employees or people involved. Employees are made aware of the required outcome, however, they are invited to be a more active part of the process. Unfortunately, soliciting feedback and encouraging inclusion can also be confusing. Sometimes these employees will think your solicitation of their feedback indicates your willingness to bend to disapproving opinions and change the path. In other words, abandon your project and go back to the way things were. Because, if they are not in agreement, that will be the decision driver for continuing, right? Wrong! Feedback can help us overcome obstacles that we may encounter on the path to improvement, but feedback should not determine whether or not we stay on the path. It might be velvet, but it is still a hammer.

Photo: Gennady

Volunteers are a special category, and sometimes even a "velvet hammer" is too harsh when working with volunteers. Volunteers are encouraged when they experience successful outcomes and feel appreciated. Being hit with a hammer, velvet or otherwise, doesn't typically foster a feeling of success or appreciation.

This is why process improvement in a volunteer environment can be tricky. The "velvet hammer" can be used to gently nudge volunteers to develop new strategies. Unfortunately, the implementation timeline has to fit the volunteer's availability. In addition to availability, continual turnover of volunteers can impede the ability to reach a timely completion. This is precisely why volunteer-based non-profits can remain stagnant for decades.

Selling the idea of improvement

What's in it for us? This question should always be asked when process improvement is considered, and will be asked by management. Count on it! There are two ways to answer the question:

1. Calculated Outcomes
   Calculated outcomes are quantifiable predictable outcomes that support your process improvement effort. Typically, a calculated improvement will result in the savings of a specific number of dollars, or increase production by a specific percentage point. Calculated outcomes often require a fair amount of data analysis and research to be able to identify those specific numbers, prior to getting started.

2. Intended Outcomes
   Intended outcomes are supported by logic and realistic assumptions (common sense).

A process improvement project proposing to hire an additional call center staff member predicting a decrease of overall call times by 45 seconds is an example of a calculated outcome. There is stress around calculated outcomes, though. What if you hire your staff and the overall call time only decreases by 30 seconds. Yes, it's still an improvement, but the project failed to meet its calculated outcome. That could be a costly failure for a company whose call center expense is thousands of dollars per minute. A company like this would want to know the exact outcomes they can expect, and that is why more complicated, data driven protocols exist.

A similar improvement project might propose hiring an additional call center staff member citing decreased overtime, lower call center times, and improved morale as the project improvement objectives. Intended outcomes are rarely aligned with specific numbers, percentages or dollars. It is reasonable, however, to assume that the introduction of additional staff will alleviate pressure being experienced by current staff.

Intended results represent the majority of process improvement efforts. Primarily because most companies lack the expertise and resources to support the complexity of calculated outcomes, nor can they justify the time required to gather and analyze the data necessary to predict those calculated outcomes. Because this book is focused on a more manageable approach to process improvement, the examples and case studies will point to intended results.

CHAPTER 1
Diagnosis: Broken
"A delusion is something that people believe in, despite a total lack of evidence."
- Richard Dawkins

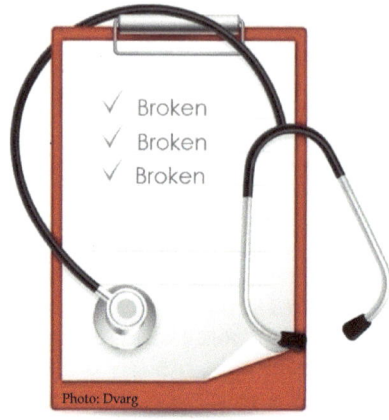

✓ Broken
✓ Broken
✓ Broken

Photo: Dvarg

The first step to beginning a process improvement project is diagnosing a process as broken. This may seem elementary, but there are delusional institutions we deal with daily that have broken processes, and yet nobody in a position of authority is willing to use the "B" word – "Broken." Take healthcare for example. Have you ever sat on hold for a ridiculous amount of time, been given information that makes no sense, had funds or access to care withheld, only to hear… "Is there anything else I can help you with today?" Does your frustration skyrocket along with your blood pressure? Of course it does! Yet there is no acknowledgement that something is broken on the other end of the line. Without that acknowledgement, it is tough to move forward with improvement.

Diagnosing brokenness is a symptomatic process. Jeff Foxworthy, a famous comedian, has made us all experts on what it means to be a "Redneck" with his joke series "You might be a redneck if…" We laugh at the humor, but Mr. Foxworthy is pointing out that there are some obvious observations that can be made that equal "Redneck." I think we can do the same thing with brokenness.

• **Something might be broken if… Unhappiness is common among internal and external customers.**

External customers are those individuals that purchase your product or utilize your service.

- Do social media reviews, surveys, and customer service calls reflect that customers are dissatisfied as they interact with you or your company?

- Are sales declining?

Internal customers are employees, and can sometimes include vendors or anyone that might be leveraged to create your product or deliver your service.

- Are employees unhappy?

- Is there grumbling and gossiping, turnover, and broken contracts?

- Have otherwise pleasant hires become frustrated and irritable?

- **Something might be broken if... Goals don't get met or tasks don't get completed.**

Do deadlines keep getting pushed out with no end in sight?

- **Something might be broken if... Processes aren't completed right the first time around.**

"Re-dos" are costly. How often do things have to be re-done, re-created, or re-manufactured?

Has accommodating the "re-do" become a culture of the business?

- **Something might be broken if... People and/or money are thrown at the problem, yet the problem persists.**

Are people and funds allocated without an expectation of outcomes?

Do employees churn around projects that never deliver?

- **Something might be broken if... Processes span several departments resulting in finger-pointing and blaming.**

Is there an owner of the process, or has the responsibility been so scattered that multiple employees and departments can easily shed accountability?

Is the process handed off to numerous individuals allowing opportunity for failure?

- **Something might be broken if... Outcomes are not measured or controlled.**

How is success defined and how does the organization ensure that the solution is going to stick over time?

- **Something might be broken if... Data redundancy is rampant.**

  How many times is the same information entered or reviewed?

  How many systems (that don't talk to each other) are required, making data inconsistent or inaccurate?

- **Something might be broken if... Too many reviews/sign-offs are required.**

  Is it tough to gain traction because you have to stop at every manager's door for approval?

  In a world where communication is immediate, how long does it take to get a return email, a clarification, or an approval?

  How much time is spent waiting for the direction necessary to move forward? As you wait, do efforts grow stagnant while focus gets redirected to other priorities?

- **Something might be broken if... Complexity, exceptions & special cases are common.**

  How often is the term "custom" used when trying to avoid processes and procedures?

  Are standard operating procedures difficult to nail down because everything is "custom?"

- **Something might be broken if... Established procedures are circumvented to expedite work.**

  When critical deadlines quickly approach, do existing policies and procedures get thrown out the window?

  Does panic around unreasonable or unachievable deadlines also drive bad decisions and flawed judgement?

- **Something might be broken if... Inventory sits idle.**

  Do your products or service struggle to make their way out the door?

- **Something might be broken if… Procedures are passed on by word of mouth.**

  Has tribal knowledge become the culture? When someone gets sick, goes on vacation, or leaves, is the organization lost due to lack of documentation.

  Is recreating the wheel a standard response to turnover?

  Does the culture foster a sense of "job security" through knowledge held tightly in the heads of individual employees?

- **Something might be broken if… Firefighting is admired.**

  Is there one crisis after another, leaving little time for innovation?

  Are the crisis handlers often rewarded?

You might be experiencing brokenness if any of these symptoms are present.

CHAPTER 2
So, Why Don't We "Un-Break" It?

"He that is good for making excuses is seldom good for anything else."
— Benjamin Franklin

Photo: Jacek

Is it enough to know something is broken? You might know your lawn mower is broken, but that knowledge alone doesn't maintain the lawn. Simply acknowledging that your glass is broken, does not make it safe for drinking. A willingness to go beyond acknowledgement and into action is required to make something better. However, there are key reasons why we don't move into action, a bulk of which have to do with fear.

The fear that it must be <u>MY FAULT</u> it's broken.

Implementing a fix is avoided when we don't want anyone to perceive that we have failed. After all, if something needs to be fixed, it's because it's broken, and if it's broken, it must mean that somebody did something wrong or somebody wasn't doing their job. We can't spell FAIL<u>U</u>RE without "U" ("you"), right?

Wrong! Nevertheless, this jams up a lot of organizations. If we are being honest, it's painful when a process we have spent years developing and fostering is no longer performing. Maybe we hear words like inefficient, costly, time consuming, or frustrating. Nobody likes to hear their hard work described this way, and it's difficult not to take it personally. Broken processes often make employees protective and defensive.

Overcoming this hurdle is critical if any process is to be improved. The reasons that a process no longer works is more likely because the organization has outgrown it, resources have grown or diminished, the economy has experienced an extreme shift, or technology has hit us at the speed of light. These very real reasons have nothing to do with personal incompetence.

Social security is a great example of a process that worked well, originally! Changing resources, economy, and expectations over time, make it ripe for improvement; none of these issues are Franklin D. Roosevelt's fault. Have you ever needed treatment in a hospital during a nursing shortage? The processes put in place when they were fully staffed aren't necessarily going to work well when the nursing staff is reduced by 50%. That doesn't mean the developer of the process is at fault.

In order to make things better, we must let go of the pride and ownership linked to broken processes.

The fear there's <u>NOTHING IN IT FOR ME!</u>
This is a big one. Most employees, especially hourly employees, will stay clear of process improvement because in all honesty, there is no motivation. Are they going to get paid more if the improvement is a success, and paid less if it fails? Is the reward of a promotion being dangled, or the threat of being fired being wielded? Why embark on the perceived hassle if there is "nothing in it for me!"

In order to make things better, there must be a personal motivation. Expecting the "feel good" associated with doing the right thing to be that motivator can sometimes be disappointing.

The fear that the problem is <u>TOO BIG TO SOLVE.</u>
It's very easy to be overwhelmed by the entirety of an issue. It's even easier to slip into the dysfunctional thinking that the problem is too huge and any attempt at improvement will be futile. If it won't be enough to solve the WHOLE problem, why bother?

How many professions out there are NOT expected to solve the whole problem? Look at a Firefighter. A Firefighter might not be able to save the structure, but when he/she rescues the people and the family pets, we call that successful! A surgeon may not have saved the limb, but they saved the life! We are good with that! Compromises are part of process improvement. Sometimes problems are too big to solve all at once, and professionals have to be willing to take it in bite-sized pieces.

Take American politics as an example, again. Term limits, spending, partisanship, pork-barrel legislation, filibusters, corruption, and the list goes on! What might we be able to accomplish if we just focused on say, term limits. If we fixed one aspect of the brokenness and then re-evaluated, might we find that some of the other issues disappear? We will never know if we don't start somewhere.

In order to make things better, we must be willing to compromise and accept that some success is better than no success.

The fear we will MAKE THINGS WORSE.
If we try to solve the problem, we could be jumping from the frying pan into the fire!!!

We've all seen it happen. Someone sets out to do something noble and it ends up worse. Everyone had gotten comfortable with the broken pieces, because everyone knew where the broken pieces were. But when someone tried to fix it, they moved all the pieces and now life has gotten worse. Nobody wants "made things more painful" as their legacy.

The number of students required to take remedial courses before entering college has grown year over year, all because someone wanted to improve math and reading scores. It happens, and the prospect of being "that guy" scares us into process improvement paralysis.

In order to make things better, we must be open to the possibility that wrong steps can happen. But if we don't give up, wrong steps can help us find the right direction.

The fear the solution WILL COST TOO MUCH.
We know what the cost is for the process in its current state of brokenness. Can we afford to fix it? The fear that we are going to spend more money fixing a problem than the problem itself costs, can also be paralyzing. Unknown dollars combined with unknown outcomes is risky business, and the risk could be someone's job. Not many will raise their hand for that opportunity.

Those of us who lived in Colorado in the 80s remember the building of Denver International Airport ("DIA"). One of the design elements of the airport was a state-of-the-art baggage handling system. This system was fully automated and was intended to take the place of many, if not all, baggage handling employees.

It was a disaster. Year after year, bags were late, missing or demolished. The broken system became the "black eye" of DIA. The baggage handling system was a significant reason that the airport was delayed 16 months in opening and was over budget by 500 Million dollars. How long do you have to suffer with a debacle like this before cost isn't a factor? How about 10 years? Living with the pain was a conscious choice, and it took 10 years of torture before the powers that be could financially justify making it better.

In order to make things better we must recognize that sometimes there will be a cost involved.

The fear that solving the problem will go against the culture, because WE LIKE THINGS BROKEN.

Yes, organizations will leave things broken because they like it that way. Organizations can become comfortable with the brokenness. Embracing crisis, frustration, and fire drills can just become part of the culture. It is the definition of normal in many organizations, and they don't know how to run things differently. Employees consider the term "firefighters" a badge of honor, because they excel at it. It makes them feel valuable, useful, and secure. But beware! If an organization rewards firefighting, they may also be encouraging arsonists. In this environment, there isn't a great use for planners, builders or developers. You have to either be a firefighter or an arsonist to survive. Employees in the middle typically get burned!

I shared a work environment with an employee that went out of his way to create conflict. I could feel my stomach seize daily as I neared the office, knowing that a confrontation was inevitable. Sometimes, I would even hold onto items that required interacting with this person until I felt confident about my ability to fight back. It was ridiculous! One day, we got into it. It was epic. When he stormed off, my supervisor's boss came over and put her hand on my shoulder and said, "Good job!"

That's it! "Good job!" Why didn't she step in? Why didn't she lead and manage a resolution. Turmoil caused by this individual had become entertainment, and the explosions were now part of the acceptable culture. When I decided to sit down with the employee and make peace, I was accused of being a traitor. Since when does making peace equal traitor? Making peace equals traitor when making peace puts out the fire that others now find comfortable and familiar to huddle around.

In order to make things better, sometimes culture must be examined and redefined.

The fear that the situation is WAY TO RISKY.

Every process improvement project will have a level of fear and a level of risk, from fear of failure to risk of unemployment or damaged professional reputation.

Process Improvement is assertive, aggressive, stringent, confrontational, and RISKY. What does the level of risk tell us? Can we work with the risk, rather than letting it cripple progress? Risk makes us stop and ask questions. Risk makes us pause. Risk is a part of every decision we make, and not necessarily a bad thing.

The higher the risk, the more planning, money and time we can expect to spend. This is why homework is essential. We better know what we're doing when risk is high. But when the risk is low, there is less planning, less money and less time required to make things better. When the risk is low, we should ask ourselves, "What do we have to lose?"

During an Infant CPR course, one of the students posed a question. She had heard that if you press too hard, you could break little ribs. She wanted to know how to avoid breaking ribs because she didn't want to **hurt** the baby she was trying to help. The instructor stopped and walked around the table and asked everyone to pay close attention. "Ma'am," he said, "that baby is dead! You can't hurt them more than dead. Do the compressions and don't worry about the ribs! It's better to be alive and have a couple of broken ribs, than to be dead with all your ribs intact! Don't you think?" His point was "Doing something is better than doing nothing – when dead is what you're starting with." This applies to processes. If the process or progress is dead, there is no risk of making it worse. For Pete's sake, try something!

In order to make something better we must embrace some level of risk. After all, even if we are falling on our face... we are falling forward and gaining ground.

The fear that <u>SIMPLE CAN'T BE MEANINGFUL.</u>
This is where I sigh, heavily! Because, this is where I hear, "Go Big or Go Home!" If it's not huge, then it's not worthwhile. If it doesn't fall into the category of high profile, high budget, and high risk, then it can't possibly be meaningful. I have personally worked with a process improvement team that required a year to determine the scope of a problem. For some protocols, like Six Sigma, the research can require multiple staff members, dedicated solely to gathering data to then be able to identify the problem. Sometimes, if we look closer, what we think is a single problem actually morphs into many problems, and requires many solutions.

Let's face it! Few people have the time for such a long and drawn out project. Can a problem actually be improved easily? Can the improvement be simple? In more instances than not, a small, simple improvement is what's needed to make any progress at all.

My husband and I took on the task of laying 700 SF of floor tile. A task worth every penny a professional might charge. We have all learned that parallel lines remain equal distances apart. But if one line is angled, even the slightest amount, the distance between the lines will continue to grow. Yes, this is what happened with our tile. By the time we got to the last quarter of the project, the distance between each tile was embarrassing! The same thing happens with our process improvements, but in a good way. We travel the same path, day after day, and disregard the value of small, purposeful pivots in direction. When small deviations are made, the difference between where we were, and where we are going, grows exponentially over time.

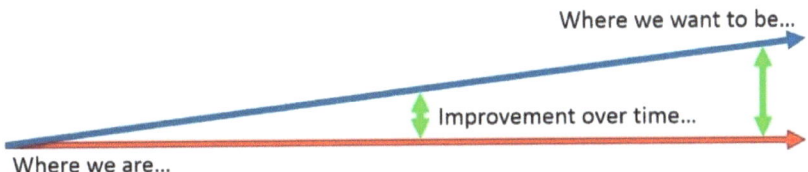

That is why "low hanging fruit" is such an important consideration. For those that have never heard the term "low hanging fruit," think of it this way... the most obvious problems that are hanging right in front of our face, and within your capability and authority to improve. These are problems that don't require wading through layers of approvals, have no real budget requirements, and don't need additional staff. You might think, "Those improvements can't possibly be impactful!" I attest, "Yes they can! In order to make things better, sometimes we must first consider those improvements that are within our grasp.

As we dive into the steps required for a successful process improvement project, remember that "low hanging fruit" does not imply that you can skip steps and jump to solutions. Instead these types of improvements represent projects that may not take as much time as they go through the steps. Don't skip steps, ever, no matter how low the fruit hangs!

CHAPTER 3
Deciding Which Pain to Ease

"Pain insists upon being attended to."
- C.S. Lewis

Hear It – Ease It – Erase It

There will be no shortage of feedback when a group of employees, volunteers, or family members get together to discuss what causes them pain. Once the conversation gets going, the list will be long. There will always be issues, processes, and people that cause frustration. How do you decide which frustration is worthy of your time and effort to improve?

We have to be realists! Not every pain can be erased, or even eased. If we focus on issues that can't be improved, we waste time, money, and energy. Instead, let's spend our time wisely on issues where we can confidently make positive improvements.

Every issue fits into one of three categories, based on one fundamental factor – how much authority do you actually have to improve this situation?

  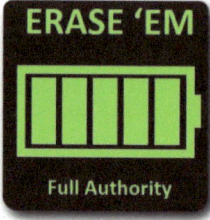

Hear 'Em Category
You have no authority whatsoever over the issue.

This category is a favorite of the gripers and whiners. They are folks who stand at the water cooler every day and complain about the size of their cubicle or the amount taken out of the check for insurance premiums.

These are issues that typically are chronic in nature, but cannot be impacted in any way by you, or anyone in your immediate circle feeling the same pain. All we can do is hear these complaints. Once we have heard the frustrations about things we cannot change, we must let them go. If we don't, they will become distractions on the pathway to progress, or barriers to other improvement opportunities in the pipeline.

Ease 'Em Category
You typically have some authority, or if you personally have no authority, someone on your team has a level of authority.

These are issues that can be improved, but most likely not completely eradicated. If we are to focus on these issues, we must be prepared to compromise, because we may not be able to get rid of all of the pain points or meet all of the objectives. But we can make things better by easing some of the pain points and achieving some of the objectives.

For the "go big or go home" thinkers who will only be interested in the all or nothing fix, this category is a tough pill to swallow. They will need to be educated and coached on the power of the small deviation over time, or the power of consecutive problem solving which addresses pieces of the problem over time.

Erase 'Em Category
You typically have full authority.

These are issues that we are confident can be completely erased from our world. Of course we should make them disappear if we can. However, this can be a deceiving category. Often times we think we can solve the issue completely, and are disappointed when we find out that we cannot.

As you go through your pain points, it will be interesting to see where your team members place the pain. Don't be surprised when a pain you feel can be eased, others may feel can only be heard.

CHAPTER 4
"Un-Breaking It!" It's Elementary!

"If you can't explain it to a six year old, you don't understand it yourself."
— Albert Einstein

I have a recipe for pumpkin bars that is out of this world. Even people who hate pumpkin, love my pumpkin bars. Entire pans of bars have gone missing, pan and all, out of fear that a department might not get their fill. An inch of dense pumpkin, and about 2 inches of fluffy cream cheese goodness. Out of this world!

I have never withheld the recipe from anyone who has asked for it. I am happy to share the joy; however, I make sure the person requesting the recipe understands that the ingredients must be slowly added, in the order given. Without fail, the baker will come back to me and say, "Mine didn't taste like yours!" I will ask if they added the ingredients in the order given, slowly one ingredient at a time, with a mixer. At this point I will hear excuses about being busy, not having the right tools, missing ingredients, etc. In other words, they didn't follow the recipe. So why are they always so surprised when they don't get the same result?

Process improvement is very much like my pumpkin bar recipe. All the ingredients are required to be added, and in the order listed. If you don't, you may not get the desired result – which is improvement!

R E C I P E S

For: Process Improvement

Ingredients:
- **Insight** *
- **Planning** *
- **Action** *
- **Oversight** *

Directions:
Whip up some insight, mix it with planning. Bake it into action and frost it with oversight.

* These ingredients are rarely available "off the shelf." You may have to create them from "SCRATCH."

From the Kitchen of : Administrative Architects

Photo: Eros Erika

Phase 1: Insight – Make sure you have some!

I need to start this segment by communicating the importance of this phase. Insight is critical to laying the foundation for a good process improvement project. The temptation to jump from pain to resolution will be intense, and making that mistake will rarely give the result you seek.

Insight is the capacity to gain an accurate and deep intuitive understanding. Nobody, and I mean nobody, gains insight from focusing solely on their own experiences and knowledge. Insight requires the inclusion of information outside our personal frame of reference. The "Insight" phase will include the following:

- **Step One: Engage Your Stakeholders**
  If only we could improve our situations on our own! Well, we can't! A stakeholder is anyone that can affect the outcome, or be impacted by your process improvement project. If you don't get the buy-in from your stakeholders, your improvement will not be well received, and may even be rejected – even if your improvement is a good one. More importantly, if you don't get your stakeholder's feedback, you may end up attacking the wrong problem.

  Gaining insight from stakeholders can include inviting them into the process via team meetings, surveys, one-to-one conversations, or focus groups. Stakeholders, once identified, are a critical part of working through the entire process of making something better. They may observe and experience pain associated with the problem you didn't even know existed. They may know information that paints an entirely different picture than the one you see. The most meaningful, long lasting improvement endeavors always include the feedback of Stakeholders and their position within the project.

  Stakeholders can be:
    - Boss/Supervisor
    - Co-workers
    - Subordinates
    - Vendors
    - Clients
    - Family
    - Friends
    - Volunteers

Beware of the stakeholder who knows just enough to be dangerous. Without fail, there will always be a stakeholder who will challenge an improvement effort by throwing out a term like Six Sigma or Lean, and insisting on utilizing these more established and profound protocols. Let me start by saying that process improvement is a refined skill. The protocols like Six Sigma and Lean are amazing in the way they enable a group to drill down into the details and draw logical and defendable conclusions with predictable outcomes. Unfortunately, it is common that the person(s) throwing out the suggestion to use the protocols, may know just enough about them to be dangerous, and that can derail your improvement efforts. These protocols only work well if the people using them have the skill and knowledge to use them correctly, and the authority to allocate the funds necessary to implement their recommendations.

Taking one of these protocols, like Six Sigma or Lean, and adding assumptions, short cuts, and misinterpretations can be detrimental to outcomes; for example:

Elementary Schools in our District were old and neglected... and built with no air conditioning. This may have been acceptable decades before when the schools were built, however, teachers in the late 90s were quitting or retiring early because they could not take the heat. When a new Elementary School was built just a mile away with building-wide air conditioning and a fireplace in the cafeteria, a couple of parents were done being overlooked. Yes, I am talking about myself and one other mom – shout out to my teammate! We put our heads together and began to solve the problem, as we saw it, in a manner that we thought exhibited a great deal of reason and common sense. That was our first mistake! We knew there was never going to be funding, so we approached local business owners who agreed to donate the money to purchase a window air conditioner for each room of the school. Another vendor agreed to install them at no charge. All of this could be done over the summer break. Cool, huh?

Of course, the school administration was not agreeable to such a simple, low cost, low effort solution. They even said if we got the units installed, we would not be permitted to plug them in. You see, they could not allow us to improve the school beyond the other schools in the same class in the same district. I know, crazy! What they did say was that they would put together a Six Sigma team to properly address the issue. They explained that this protocol would allow them to adequately evaluate the situation and come up with a solution that was supported by data. This was the first time we had heard of Six Sigma, and with the term being foreign to us at the time, we went with it.

The school proceeded to use SIX employees (because they told us it required 6 employees because it's SIX Sigma – of course) over SIX months (again with the SIX) to come up with SIX possible solutions. (Is anyone else seeing 6-6-6 here?)

Over $10,000 was spent on an environmental consultant who was to provide the data. The data they ultimately provided was that the school maintained a number of degrees above the acceptable degree for optimal learning. In other words, "IT'S HOT IN THERE." One of the solutions recommended decreasing the temperature by installing a ceiling mounted air conditioning system for the entire building. Perfect! Now that we have a recommendation, backed by indisputable data, when can we get the system installed? Oh, we can't! Why? There is no money!!! Instead we were informed that the District would be looking into painting the air vents white under each classroom window, to help deflect the heat.

At this point, I needed someone to explain to me this Six Sigma thing! My $3 thermometer from Lowes read a temperature of 103 in the music room, and this low-tech item came to the same conclusion as the high priced environmental consultant. Adding insult to injury, the vents never did get painted.

You are probably curious as to if and when a solution was ever implemented? When the Superintendent attempted to pass a Mill Levy and Bond a year later, he recognized that our force of "two" still existed and we would successfully damage his campaign. He promised to make our neighborhood school the first in line to receive improvements if the Bond/Mill passed, which included air conditioning. In the end, good ole "strong-arming" ended up being the winning strategy!

These individuals didn't know Six Sigma, and they didn't have the funding and authority to implement any recommendations the Six Sigma process might yield. The result was a lot of wasted taxpayer money, diverted time and energy, and loss of confidence, all because people simply didn't know what they were doing.

It is important to note that even large companies which adopt, teach, and support Six Sigma and Lean don't always get it right. One such company approached their Six Sigma team and explained that the budget for the upcoming year was completed based on a decrease in call times within the call center. I was a part of that Six Sigma team and we were instructed to put together a Six Sigma project to reduce call times resulting in the financial savings to match the budget. Ummm.... that's not how it works. The Six Sigma project will tell you if the call times are a problem, and if so, what reasonable reduction in call time could be achieved providing certain improvements were made. As it turned out, the reduction being asked for was an impossibility, although the budget was never adjusted to reflect reality.

So what is Six Sigma? I'll save you the Google search. In 1986, a couple of engineers from Motorola introduced Six Sigma as a disciplined, data-driven approach and methodology for eliminating defects (driving toward **six** standard deviations between the mean and the nearest specification limit) in any process – from manufacturing to transactional and from product to service. Yes, it's complicated.

Anyone who has been trained in Six Sigma, and used it in business, knows that it is reasonable to expect it to take a year to develop a problem statement. There are some companies that generate billions in product or revenue, and if they are making a shift, they darn well better make sure the shift is in the right direction. News flash... this is a certification, a degree, an education career path! Your team is not going to become fluent in the understanding and use of these protocols during a 60 minute conference call or because one member read a Facebook article. Any attempt to utilize these protocols on a stakeholder's book knowledge is crazy, and if you allow them, these stakeholders will take you on a one-way trip into Crazyville!

The average company with the average employees have processes to improve, and need something simpler!

It is unlikely anyone on your stakeholder team represents the level of expertise, and equally important the availability, required to work a true Six Sigma or Lean project.

Be prepared, as the project leader, to take a stand with your stakeholders in support of a simpler approach.

- **Step Two: Make Observations**
  People who impose perceived solutions without insight can be scary, and a little time spent in observation could be a game changer. Walk in someone else's shoes for a day. Step through their frustrations with them and observe how those around react. This is the step where you understand the history of the problem and the data around the pain. Witnessing what is happening for yourself can be priceless!

- **Step Three: Develop a Problem Statement**
  Every process improvement effort must begin with a problem statement. A problem statement is a specific statement that identifies the problem, without including symptoms or implying solutions. If a problem statement cannot be identified, an improvement cannot be implemented. If an improvement strategy is implemented without a clear problem statement, chances are good that the problem will not be improved.

  Being specific is key when building a problem statement. General and ambiguous terms can derail any attempt at improvement. A problem statement does not need to be long. As a matter of fact, the longer it gets, the more misleading it will become.

  A good problem statement is the byproduct of stakeholder feedback, observations, history, and data. What is really happening; not what you think is happening, but true data. Even if you suspect you know what the solution might be, don't be tempted to incorporate it into the problem statement.

  - Vague/misleading problem statement:
    My car won't start.

    Good problem statement:
    When I put the key in the ignition, my car won't start.

  - Vague/misleading problem statement:
    My baby never stops crying.

    Good problem statement:

Within 5 minutes of eating, my baby cries for at least 2 hours.

"Never stops crying" is an absolute and "car won't start" is quite vague. What if the reason your car won't start is because you grabbed the wrong keys? A few details, like when it happens and duration can help eliminate spending time on the wrong solutions.

- Vague/misleading problem statement:
  We can't seem to hire the right people to get the job done.

  Good problem statement:
  We have missed the completion deadlines on 7 of the last 9 projects.

  "We can't seem to hire the right people" implies that you already know why the job can't get done – bad employees. A predetermined cause will most definitely predetermine a solution, which may be wrong.

- Vague/misleading problem statement:
  We need to send more emails so our members know what's going on.

  Good problem statement:
  80% of our members don't attend events.

  More emails may improve attendance, or it may not. Maybe they just don't like your event content. If that's the case, all the emails in the world aren't going to entice their attendance.

- Vague/misleading problem statement:
  Our call response time needs to be better to make our customers happier.

  Good problem statement:
  Customer satisfaction has declined, month over month, in the last 10 months.

  Long call times are a symptom of the problem, which is customer satisfaction. Don't impose a solution, because at this point, customer service could be easily impacted by something you haven't even considered yet.

- **Step Four: Rank Symptoms and Objectives**
  Now that you have leveraged your stakeholders, performed practical observation, and developed your problem statement, it's time to look a little deeper into what the symptoms of this problem are, and what objectives you hope to achieve. Don't be stingy about the symptoms. Hold a brainstorm session and list all of the thoughts and ideas, in whatever order they are mentioned. Stakeholders must contribute to this list for a complete understanding.

  Once the symptoms are identified, the objectives can then be revealed. As a collective group, you and your stakeholders will determine what you hope to accomplish.

  Ranking is critical. Your improvement may not be able to address all the symptoms. You want to make certain that if you implement a process improvement strategy, you are clear about what symptom and objective you are trying to achieve. Additionally, if you are able, address the symptom and meet the objective ranked the highest.

  Your team can make lists, but I like to keep this as simple as possible by using a table that allows me to list symptoms in the left column, objectives in the center column, and ranking in the right column. In this format, you can align symptoms and objectives, and then rank, all in one.

Symptom	Objective	Rank
Legally non-compliant	Legally compliant	1
Negative morale	Positive morale	2

One additional consideration when gaining insight: The time you spend observing the situation, talking with stakeholders, and developing your problem statements will vary. On one issue there may be nothing to observe, but lots of stakeholder input. On another issue, you might spend more time observing with minimal stakeholder input. Be flexible, each process improvement project will present different levels of insight in different areas.

Phase 2: Plan; Improvement Doesn't Happen On a Whim!

- **Step One: Identify Your Resources**

= RESOURCES

Resources = Money + People + Time. It is important to know your resources before you start entertaining improvements. If you have unlimited funds with a lot of people, you don't need as much time. If you don't have money, but you have a few people, it may take more time. If you have no money and no people, be very reasonable about deadlines. Don't entertain improvement strategies your <u>present</u> resources cannot support.

I've been to a number of sales and leadership conferences, and my least favorite exercise is, "If money and staff were no object, what would you like to see happen?" This always ranks as the biggest waste of time, because money and people are always factors. To attempt a process improvement project without respect for resources is to entertain disappointment.

- **Step Two: Document Your Exclusions and Limitations**
Here is where we have to be honest about what we will NOT do! What problems are we NOT going to address in this endeavor? What money are we NOT going to spend, and what people are we NOT going to leverage?

This is important because if we don't define what we won't do, we will end up doing it. When that happens, we will engage in what's known as "scope creep." We end up adding things we didn't intend, and focusing on complaints that are not relevant to our original issue. More resources will be required, and ultimately, your effort may never get off the ground, or worse yet, may be seen as unsuccessful. Know what you won't do.

- **Step Three: Evaluate Potential Improvement Strategies, Risks, and Oversight Requirements**

Now it's time to entertain the possible improvement strategies which best address the problem. This is an area where balls get dropped with process improvement. It is so tempting to implement a strategy before the necessary due diligence. It is work to get to this point.

Make a list of the ways you might be able to make the situation better. I call these improvement strategies. Don't be stingy.

For each strategy proposed, there may be a risk. If there is, ask yourself these questions:

- Is the risk acceptable?
- Do you have the resources to pull of the improvement?
- Is the current staffing sufficient in number and skillset?
- How is the improvement going to be effective over time?
- Does it need management oversight to be effective month over month?
- Is it an improvement strategy that needs no oversight?
- Will it require training?
- Will one training session be enough or will multiple training sessions over time be required to ensure the positive outcomes related to this improvement?

Do not underestimate the importance of oversight and exploring it right here at this stage of the game. Most process improvements require an oversight of some kind. I think a great example of oversight, or lack thereof, is evident in some very popular Cable TV shows where a top chef/restauranteur gets invited into a completely broken restaurant or bar. They point out all of the flaws, usually using the "hammer" method, and lay out a design for the business to flourish. Although the show ends with the owner and employees grateful for the improvements and committed to keep the changes going, the follow-up data on their websites show many of the businesses fail not long after filming. Why? Because there is no oversight to make sure that people do not boomerang back into bad habits. A compulsion to go back to the old way should be expected, and even anticipated. That is why oversight is essential. If the oversight required is complicated, long lasting, and resource intensive, the improvement strategy may have to be discarded as a consideration.

- **Step Four: Make a Final Improvement Strategy Selection**

  Again, I am a fan of simple. A grid can help you be efficient and effective in the process. List your objectives in the left column, and list your strategies in the subsequent columns. As you compare your objectives to the strategy, do you think that this strategy will meet the objective? Adding some color coding, red for objective not met, yellow for objective might be met, and green for objective met, will even make it easier to identify the obvious winner.

Objectives (listed in order of importance from Step 2)	Strategy #1	Strategy #2	Strategy #3 WINNER
#1 Objective	No	Maybe	Yes
#2 Objective	No	Maybe	Yes
#3 Objective	Maybe	Maybe	Yes

Now that all of the possible improvement strategies are in front of you and your team, you will be able to identify the best strategy by reviewing your objectives and weighing them against the strategies your team identified as viable. If you have done your homework, the best option will be clear.

Phase 3: Action!
It's Time to Roll Up Our Sleeves and Get to Work!

- **Step One: Define Responsibilities & Communicate Deadlines**
  Many teams get to this point and stall. The best way to avoid stalling is to make your team of resources and stakeholders a part of the implementation plan. Give them a job!

  BEGIN WITH THE END! When do you want the improvement strategy implemented? Put a calendar in front of your team and mark your deadline. Work backwards from your deadline detailing the tasks that will be necessary in order to implement your improvement. Assign tasks and make sure your team understands that there are one-way gates and critical hand-offs.

One-way Gate: The point in the process where you can no longer go backwards. This is the point where previous decisions made are no longer able to be reversed without critically impacting deadlines and outcomes.

A video project would be a great example of a project with a one-way gate. First you decide what the topics are, then you decide who will be in the video. Finally, you identify a location for taping. The decision on topic is a one-way gate, because if you invite someone to be in the video and you give them a topic, it will become detrimental to the project if you keep changing the topic.

Critical Hand-off: Think of this like handing off a baton during a race. Runner #2 can't get going unless Runner #1 hands off the baton. Likewise, some tasks have to be completed before others can be started. An example of a critical hand-off would be if I were planning a big event and needed to order invitations. I would need the date and venue identified before I could place my order. The task of contracting the venue is necessary to then hand-off the information to the invitation designer. If I can't seem to nail down the venue, the event could be compromised because my guests may not get the invitation in time. I might even have to change the date.

- **Step Two: Adopt a Tool to Support Improvement**
  Don't bring a knife to a gun fight! Bring a gun to a gun fight, and when you do, be sure you know how to properly use it. Very few improvements will be made without leveraging a tool. A tool is a device or implement used to carry out a particular function.

Tools are a powerful component in a successful process improvement project. Tools can be forms, databases, spreadsheets, applications, presentations, and the list goes on. Tools can also be additional staff. Tools aren't always tangible. Tools can be training/coaching, mentoring, reviews, and team meetings/retreats.

> I was contracted in the mid-90s to help solve a problem at a posh design center. For those that don't know what a design center is, it is a really fancy shopping center. Buyers must be accompanied by an interior designer to enter. The inventory is so expensive and exclusive that only about 2% of the population can afford to shop there. When I was contracted, I was told that calls were coming in from tenants and designers regarding the tone and unprofessional conduct that met them at

the reception desk. Management did not have the bandwidth to identify and solve the problem, so they hired me. Yes, they could have just fired the employee in an effort to solve the problem. However, implementing this solution would have not only imposed the penalty for turnover, but if it was a true process issue, throwing a different resource at it would not have changed the outcome.

I spent two days with the front desk personnel (we will call him "David"), although symptoms revealed themselves almost immediately. There was almost no oversight, as management had offices on elsewhere in the building, and he rarely saw them. It was clear that over time, David had developed an attitude of exclusion, rather than an attitude of inclusion. When only 2% of the population can afford your product, inclusion is critical. You see, David was the King of the Building Foyer; he was in charge of verifying security badges, credentials and appointment times. He had the power to grant or deny entry!

It was clear that David had an attitude problem stemming from a failure to understand the goals and outcomes related to his job. Now, you might think David was in his comfort zone with so much power, but let me assure you, he was not. If I heard once in the first couple of days, I heard 10 times, "I am so stressed out!" Being the most hated guy in the building was not what he wanted, he just didn't have the tools to make things better.

I worked with David for 90 days. Yes, 90 days. David's employer was willing to invest in making things better! During the 90 days, David went through a lot of training. Together we looked at his processes, and created some new procedures to help him be more efficient with paperwork, so that he could have more energy for people. David saw first-hand the way I handled his customers, and he also saw the reward. After a few weeks, tenants (who routinely scowled at David as they entered), were saying "Good Morning," and willingly flashing their security badge for him to see. By the end of the 90 days, David was no longer stressed out, tenants were no longer frustrated, and designers were bringing back their clients. The most important tools we used with David were training, mentoring, communication, and rewards. None of these tools were tangible!

Most process improvement projects will require some kind of tool to achieve the goal. The tough part comes in choosing the right tool, and using that tool the way it was intended. Let me give you an example. I need you to build a house. I have delivered your supplies. Now you must get started and meet a deadline for completion.

Missing Tools!
If I had delivered 2x4s and nails, with nothing else, could you get the job done? Would you fail because building a house is a bad idea? Would you fail because the nails are too blunt? Would you fail because your hands just aren't strong enough to push the nails into the wood? Of course not! You would fail because you didn't have the proper tools. I didn't provide you with a hammer! But we jump to these conclusions in life and in business all the time. The improvement must have been a bad idea, rather than, I didn't have the right tool for implementation of the improvement strategy.

Wrong Tools!
If I had delivered 2x4s, screws, and a hammer, and nothing else, could you get the job done? Would you fail because building a house was stupid in the first place? Would you fail because the screws were faulty? Would you fail because the hammer is the worst invention on the planet? Of course not! You would fail because in spite of hard work, the tool supplied was not the right tool. The house is still a good idea. Somebody needs to figure out how to get you a screwdriver or replace the screws with nails!

Right Tools – Used the Wrong Way!

What if I had delivered 2x4s, nails, and a hammer, but you had never seen or used a hammer before. What if someone spent 5 minutes with you, teaching you to use the claw side of the hammer to drive in the nails? Would you fail because building a house never made sense in the first place? Would you fail because the nails just weren't big enough? Would you fail because the hammer is a ridiculous tool? Of course not! You would fail because nobody trained you to use the hammer correctly.

I made a startling discovery when working for a Fortune 500 company earlier in my career; I was supporting a department that was charged with analyzing patient data for an entire state. The number of records could exceed millions. That's a lot of records! The analyzing took place in a tool called Microsoft Excel. After all, it was available to every employee and part of the standard software suite. Now for those of you that entered the business world in the last 10 years, let me share a fun fact. Excel is a fabulous tool, and it can do marvelous things. However, in the good ole days, Microsoft Excel would only allow 65,000 records per worksheet. So that means the records had to be split and analyzed in segments. This is not practical, not accurate, and certainly not efficient. Unfortunately, nobody on staff was familiar with Microsoft Access, another included, but not so familiar, member of the Microsoft software suite. This left them content with the struggle. When I offered to move the data into Microsoft Access, there was apprehension which quickly turned into elation. All the records were imported into one table and quickly analyzed as a whole, because Access is a relational database, not an accounting tool. A much better tool for the job!

Phase 4: Oversight – Is Our Process Actually Improving?

- **Step One: Reviewing Objectives to Measure Success**
  No, you don't get to lob your improvement over the fence and hope for the best. In order for it to be a true process improvement project, you must be able to confirm that the process is actually improving.

The easiest way to do this is to go back to the grid you created in the Plan Phase. In that grid, the objectives that you intended to address are listed. Are you experiencing the benefit of reaching those specific objectives? Your stakeholders will be able to help you understand if you are making things better or not. Talk to them and get their continued feedback.

- **Step Two: Making Sure it Sticks**
  This is where oversight really kicks into high gear. When we considered improvement strategies, we also looked at the oversight required. Should we be providing ongoing training, updating information, or holding feedback meetings?

  Oversight is a tough job. It will require a strong constitution and a passion for all of the work that has come before, as well as the outcome you know is possible. This is the phase where new habits are created, and not always willingly.

- **Step Three: What if We Aren't Seeing Improvement?**
  We are assuming the oversight defined earlier in the process is in play. If it is not, get it in place. You can't really tell if your improvement is working if you abandon the required oversight. Look at this example:

  > *Some very expensive, highly recognizable brand name hand dryers were placed in public restrooms across the nation. This solution to costly paper supplies offered an ecologically responsible alternative to killing trees, and advertised a much more sanitary method of drying one's hands – and quickly!*

  > *Recently, there was a disturbing news story about these dryers. These dryers store so much bacteria that when the user dries their hands, their hands come out dirtier when leaving the dryer than going in!*

  > *Is the dryer bad? No, they are phenomenal and do exactly what they were meant to do. The problem is in the oversight required.*

Companies who purchase and install these units did so thinking of the cost savings, but disregarded the oversight that required they must clean these units, routinely. That means they have to continually train new employees and make sure those employees are actually doing the job. The media spot did not focus on the lack of oversight by the employer, as much as they focused on the "faulty" equipment.

If your oversight is in place, and objectives are still not being met, consider the fact that improvements which may have looked so precise on paper, may not work exactly as planned in the real world. Your stakeholders, again, will be able to give you great insight as to what may not be connecting as planned. Be prepared to tweak your plan by tweaking an existing tool or adding a new tool.

It is also imperative that you know the difference between an improvement strategy needing to be tweaked and stakeholders who are simply pushing back. I call these stakeholders "Push-Backers."

In my experience, "Push-Backers" don't necessarily reveal themselves at the beginning of the improvement process, when the project is in discussion, brainstorming and planning mode. It isn't until we begin to put things into "Action" that people get really uncomfortable and the real push back starts to happen. Be aware of two kinds of "Push-Backers."

Photo: iconspro

- **The Resistant "Push-Backer":** "This is too hard!" This may be something commonly heard when implementing a new process or tool. Of course, you will ask, "Why?" A resistant "push-backer" will not be able to identify specifics, but they will be very emotional. They will say, "I don't know, it just takes too long." When the offer is presented to sit with them to add more training, they will be too busy. Do not give in to a resistant "push-backer!"

- **The Unskilled "Push-Backer":** More often than not, skill deficits can be hidden in broken processes, and it may not be until the Action or Oversight piece is implemented that gaps are revealed. This "push-backer" may not have the skillset to understand the improvement, or be able to handle the new processes that the improvement may require. This "push-backer" will respond positively to new processes, and in some cases will respond positively to training. Hopefully, you addressed skillset when you developed the oversight for this strategy☺! Unfortunately, just because you offer someone training, doesn't mean they have the capacity to learn. If the person lacks the ability to learn, a hiring shift may be required. Yes, I am absolutely suggesting that if the improvement is critical to doing business and your current staff cannot assimilate, you may have to move them or let them go to make room for staff with the required skillset.

Hopefully, you noted skill set as a risk when considering the improvement, and therefore, this shift of employment is not a shock to the business.

Do not bend to a "Push-Backer!" To start tweaking a process because someone doesn't want to be inconvenienced, or doesn't have the skillset to grow with the improvement, will most certainly take you back to square one.

Tweaking should only take place when several stakeholders report the same barrier. This is why it is so important to meet with the stakeholders frequently, especially early in the process; by doing so you will discover their pain points early on, which will allow you to tweak quickly and appropriately.

Consider a tweak to be the repair to the pavement on the road you are taking, and not the abandonment of the road altogether.

- **Step Four: Prepare for Enforcement**
  Oversight is mostly about enforcement, and enforcement is the time, effort and energy to keep an improvement progressing. Are people changing their ways? Are they using the tools, or reverting back to how it used to be done? Are people wading through the pain of change to get to the efficiency on the other side, or are they giving

up? What are the consequences if they give up? When do consequences get implemented? Making sure you understand your authority during enforcement is critical.

Enforcement is not for the weak (or someone who needs to be liked). Choose your enforcer wisely.

That's it. Let's review how all the phases work together. Gain insight, plan and put it into action. Install some oversight and then watch and listen. Is your situation improving based on the objectives you defined? If not, tweak. If they are, keep watching and keep listening, and be open for additional areas that can now be improved because you took the first step.

CHAPTER 5
What It All Looks Like in Real Life!

"People never learn anything by being told, they have to find out for themselves."
— Paulo Coelho

Life will throw us problems, and unfortunately, it will not throw us solutions. Problems will show up in every aspect of life, whether it's your home, community, or business. In order to show how this simple process for improving things works, let's dissect some real examples from all aspects of life. Follow these case studies through the steps to understand how simple improvement strategies can be. With 30 years of corporate experience, there were many stories to tell. We will start with some light-hearted examples and work our way up in complexity. My goal is that all readers will find a point in each example that is relatable.

Case Study A – The Day Care Dilemma
Phase #1 - Insight

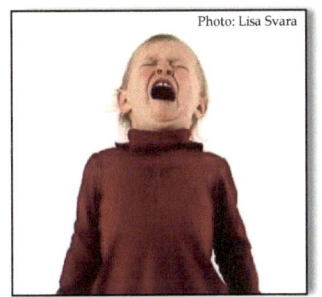
Photo: Lisa Svara

We have to go back to 1992 and visit my very short career as a daycare provider. Very short! So short that it only lasted 1 day. Don't discount this case study because you've never been a mom, or a daycare provider. This case study is really about being honest about what's really happening? I believe that message is relatable to everyone. Read on.

In 1992 I had my first child. After 8 years in the corporate world, I had made the decision to be a stay-at-home mom. However, I needed to earn a little extra cash. Daycare seemed to be the perfect solution for me… and every other Mom my age! How hard could it be, right?

Yes, I had business cards and flyers printed. I had completed all of the necessary training and certifications, and had even been approved by the State as an in-home daycare provider. I had toys, age appropriate learning curriculum, and dedicated space in the house for "daycare." I even put together a "terquarium." You saw that right, a "terquarium." That is a huge glass case that is set up like a jungle, complete with land and water creatures. Lizards lived on the dry land within the glass box, and a space was carved out in the center for the fish. The kids could peer into the world and see such great things, like lizards eating horrible, awful, itty bitty crickets and a bright blue beta fish swimming about against the glass. Woot Woot! I was ready and open for business!

Excitement was an understatement when the first call came. A woman from our church was interested in hiring me to watch her 2 year old, who we will call "Billy." My plan had paid off – an appointment was made, and Billy and his mom were going to visit my home for daycare consideration. When the doorbell rang, I greeted a 20 something mom and a cute blonde-haired, blue-eyed boy. All looked promising. They were invited in, and within minutes (it could have even been seconds) Billy had entered the playroom, turned the table upside down (to better use as a trampoline), and was screaming at the top his cute little lungs! Let's not leave out that he was pounding his fists on the "terquarium!" I could see bugs and lizards on the loose in my future. I thought, "OK, I can handle this... I can!" After a fifteen minute interview, I was hired. Well, this was easier than I thought. Billy would be joining me and my 8 week old son, tomorrow! (Yes, a 15 minute interview!)

When Billy arrived bright and early the next morning, he screamed into the house, literally. I said, "Billy! Let's wait a moment before getting into the toys." To which his mother said, "Oh, we don't tell Billy No! He is our miracle child, and we think he needs to enjoy life his own way." Seriously, I am not making this up!

Observations...
The next 10 hours were the longest 10 hours of my life. There was screaming, and punching, and spitting, and crying. Silence, joy, happiness, learning... well those things just weren't present (and I could not ever see them being present). My hope was gone in one day!
I had a problem, and it needed to be solved quickly!
So, what was the problem? Was it...

- Billy doesn't have enough discipline?
- Billy's mom needs to be a better parent?
- Toys need to be more indestructible?
- Rate for my services is not enough to attract good clients?
- I do not have adequate training?
- I do not have adequate help/staff?

Are these problems or symptoms? Are these problems or are they imposed solutions? If these are not the problem, then what is the problem? Maybe my stakeholders could shed some light on the situation.

- My husband, who shook his head when I was setting up the whole "daycare" deal, and who is anticipating some extra income.
- My son, who will learn to emulate bad behavior, every day, and who will spend all day with a miserable mom.
- My one client...

After consulting with my single most powerful stakeholder, my husband, I gained even more insight. You see, at first I thought the problem was, "I was miserable with Billy as a client." But after much discussion, he helped me to realize that this wasn't really about Billy.

You see, I am a woman of structure, and my husband was all too aware of this vice/virtue. My son had a schedule and my parenting had rules and boundaries... even at 8 weeks. My parenting style included discipline & consequences, and respect & consideration. Fundamentally, I was raising an adult and I believed allowing children to behave badly alienates them and creates adults who behave badly. It was my husband, my primary stakeholder, who introduced the idea that the problem was not Billy, or his mom, but that I just didn't like other people's out of control kids. I know that sounds horrible, but in order to improve anything, **we must be honest** about what is really happening! I am not sure I would have been as honest with myself as my stakeholder could be with me.

Problem Statement..
The problem statement ended up being "I don't like other people's kids!" Take a moment and recognize how "I don't like other people's kids" and "Billy needs more discipline" would take us down two entirely different process improvement paths. The idea that Billy is a discipline problem is part of what makes me not like other people's kids... that's a good indicator that Billy's behavior was a symptom.

Symptoms/Objectives..
What are the symptoms of my not liking other people's kids? What are the objectives related to alleviating those symptoms?

Symptom	Objective	Rank
Anxiety/Irritability *(I was miserable and it showed)*	Relaxed and Happy *(I don't want to be miserable)*	2
Destruction of property *(All the toys we had bought with our child in mind were not going to last a week.)*	Toys available for my kids *(My son should be able to have his toys free from damage, whenever he wants.)*	3
Fear of child abuse allegations *(A week with Billy and I could not trust myself!)*	Freedom from threat of jail *(A job where jail is not a clear and present possibility.)*	1

Phase #2 - Plan

Resources...

- People: How many people are available to help me improve the situation?
  - None
- Money: How much money is available to help me improve the situation?
  - None – I just spent my wad of cash setting up these shenanigans.
- Time: How much time do we have to improve the situation?
  - The timeline could be what I wanted it to be. I was the boss. However, there is still that fear of jail thing, so sooner rather than later would be best.

Exclusions/Limitations...
I will not... be hiring anyone.
I knew this going in, so it's best to establish it as an exclusion. That way no time is wasted entertaining it as a possible improvement strategy.

Improvement Strategies/Risks/Oversight.....................................

Improvement Strategy #1: Meet with Billy's Parents and develop a discipline plan.
Risk: Billy's mom will not be agreeable, or agreeable at first, and then question everything moving forward.
Oversight: A written behavior contract with daily follow-up and training. Wow! A lot of ongoing work.

Improvement Strategy #2: Invite Billy's Mom to find another provider, and only accept "well-behaved" children.
Risk: Bad reviews. Unable to find clients, or clients won't last long term. The term "bad behavior" is subjective. I am sure Billy's mom thinks his behavior is fine!
Oversight: Amend contract with behavioral requirements so the expectation is communicated up front. Enforcement would be required consistently and constantly.

Improvement Strategy #3: Stop doing daycare and find another way to make some cash.
Risk: Billy's mom will have to find another provider; Infusion of cash is delayed
Oversight: None

Does the strategy fit within the resources and exclusions and limitations? If it does, it is viable. We aren't asking if these are good ideas, yet. We are asking only if they are viable to consider.

Final Strategy

This is where we measure our process improvement strategies against our objectives. Remember that we may not be able to meet every objective. But we want to be clear about which objectives we are addressing. I recommend listing the objectives in the table with the most important at the top. (By the way, the table is a *tool*...)

Objectives (listed in order of importance from Step 2)	Strategy #1 Discipline plan for Billy	Strategy #2 Let Billy go, create contract addendum to attract better kids	Strategy #3 Stop doing daycare
Freedom from threat of Jail	No	Maybe	WINNER Yes
Relaxed and happy environment	No	Maybe	Yes
Property not destroyed	Maybe	Maybe	Yes

Phase #3 – Action

Strategy #3, "Stop Doing Daycare," officially ended my daycare career after only one day. It was the only strategy which guaranteed the achievement of my top three objectives, which I viewed as necessary to improve my situation!

Strategy #1 and #2 would have traded a number of issues which made me miserable as a daycare provider for a whole host of additional issues that would also make me miserable. These strategies would have required a whole lot of hard work, and it would not have improved the situation. Remember, the problem was that I don't like other people's kids. Strategy #1 and #2 weren't going to address that problem.

Tools

The only tool required for this strategy was communication. I called the client and let her know I would no longer be caring for her son. Business cards and flyers were promptly discarded.

Measuring Success..

Was the improvement strategy successful? Within days of implementing the strategy the threat of jail was gone, I was so much more relaxed and my belongings were not being destroyed. Yes, we achieved success based on our objectives!

Oversight..

Oddly, this is one of those process improvement strategies that required almost no oversight. We love those! I needed to put barriers in place so that I was never again lured into the delusion that working with kids was my gift. (Though I do have to say, grandkids, nieces, and nephews are a true exception to this plan, as they are permitted to break every rule in my house – with my blessing!)

PROBLEM ERASED!
INTENDED OUTCOME – SUCCESSFUL
(*The outcome was based on logic – not on dollars. Although my odds of not going to jail went from a predictable 100% to 0% overnight!*)

Case Study B: Hurried Hot Lunch

When my son was in 3rd grade, he came home from school very upset. He reported that he was starving and that he had not eaten lunch in several days. Well, you can imagine my reaction. How would this little guy get his nutrition, his eating patterns would cause digestive issues, he would be drowsy in class, and he would not be able to enjoy his much needed recess. I mean, there were all these issues that needed be addressed…. Right?

STOP… this is a great time to consider the difference between symptoms of the problem and the actual problem. A fever is a symptom of infection. If only the fever is addressed, we would miss the real problem, the infection.

Observations...
In this instance, observation seemed like the best course of action. I decided to visit the school and see for myself what this lunch situation looked like.

- Upon entering the school, I noticed that as I neared the cafetorium (that's a lunch room that doubles as an auditorium) there was a smell of wet feet! I thought, "YUK!" I wouldn't want to eat in this school either." This place needs to be cleaned!

- Then I noticed the hallway was stuffed with kids and it occurred to me that this school was overcrowded. No wonder they only got 15 minutes to eat. If only the school wasn't overcrowded, the kids could have more time to eat.

- I went in and sat down and observed the kids going through the lunch lines. They were crammed, and going back and forth, and the line was not flowing. If only we could put some professional production line principles into place here, maybe we could get this line flowing quicker.

- Then I focused on the lunch lady at the end of the line that takes the money or finds the kids in the computer. She reminded me of every trip to the DMV! You know what I am talking about – *slow motion*. If only they had a more enthusiastic, skilled, employee, they could probably get double the kids through, lickety split!

- Then I watched the mom-volunteers. They were very dedicated to their personal conversations, and if they would just pay more attention to getting these kids where they needed to be, instead of having their adult conversations in the middle of this madhouse, maybe the kids would be more focused.

- Then I looked over at my adorable son and watched as he was laughing, chatting, moving around, and NOT eating. Actually, 75% of his time was spent goofing off.

Stakeholders

- Principal
- Teachers
- Lunch Lady
- Parent Volunteers
- Students
- My son

Sometimes stakeholders cannot be addressed and included. This can happen when you don't have direct access to them, or when they just don't want to be included. In this case, most of my stakeholders had no interest in my son and his lunch problems. They had bigger fish to fry! In addition, to invite some of these stakeholders would have created more problems than it would solve. That said, we must acknowledge them, nonetheless.

If my problem statement were, My son is unable to eat... we should ask, "Why is he unable to eat?" Do his teeth hurt? Should we take him to the dentist? Is he sick? Is he allergic? This statement could easily take us down a health solutions path. But is that the right path?

Let's be a little more specific with our statement. "My son is unable to eat lunch." Ok, it's not an "eating" issue as much as an "eating lunch" issue. But why? Is he being bullied? Did he lose his lunch? Is he selling his lunch? Why just lunch? This leads us down a behavioral solution path. Is this the right path?

Do you see all the bunny trails we could go down here? By adding two words we have changed the direction of our potential improvement.

Let's be a little more specific. How about, "My son is not eating his lunch in the 15 minute time frame that all students are given." Wow, this statement just eliminated a whole host of bunny trails that now we don't even have to go down, all because we were specific and kept asking "Why?" Notice that although we have some boundaries around our problem statement, we don't offer any consequences, symptoms, reasons, or solutions.

Problem Statement: My son is not eating his lunch in the 15 minute time frame permitted.

Symptoms/Objectives...

What are the symptoms of my son not eating his lunch in the time provided? What are the objectives we hope to achieve?

Symptom	Objective	Rank
Anxiety around Lunch	Enjoy Lunch	4
Can't Enjoy Recess - Socialize	Participate in Recess/Socialize	3
Not Getting Daily Nutrition	Receive Daily Nutrition	1
Lack of focus in class at end of day	Focus on learning throughout the day	2

Note the ranking here. For me, the top priority was nutrition, the last priority was enjoyment. If I can implement a strategy that improves all four, wonderful. But in the event the strategy can only improve one objective, I need it to be one that focuses on nutrition.

Resources..

- People: How many people are available to help me improve the situation?
  - None
- Money: How much money is available to help me improve the situation?
  - None (It's a public school!)
- Time: How much time do we have to improve the situation?
  - It seems this should be addressed immediately. After all, lunch is important and he's got three years left in this school. The problem will most likely persist.

Exclusions/Limitations..

I will not...   be spending any of my own money to address this problem.
I will not...   be asking for school funds to address the problem.
I will not...   be the daily lunch babysitter.

Improvement Strategies/Risks/Oversight.......................................

There appeared to be a lot of opportunities for improvement here. If I could implement a strategy to improve them all, that would be amazing. However, with the resources I had at my disposal, (me, myself and I – and no money), that would not be possible. Instead, I was going to have to look at the issues and implement the ONE that was going to impact my objectives in the biggest way.

For the sake of argument, let's include strategies that aren't supported by our resources, just to see how they look when weighed against our objectives.

Improvement Strategy #1: The school smells like wet dirty feet. Clean the floors and carpets for a more appetizing smell.
Risk: School/Administration will not comply.
Oversight: It would need to be cleaned routinely, incurring ongoing expenses paid for by me!

Improvement Strategy #2: Address overcrowding by building more schools with more capacity.
Risk: School/Administration will not comply.
Oversight: Continual meetings with the School Board regarding funding and timing, as well as a crash course in how to be political.

Improvement Strategy #3: Redesign how the kids flow through the line and to the register.
Risk: School may not comply.
Oversight: Monitor would have to be onsite daily to manage flow. I would have to be the volunteer monitor.

Improvement Strategy #4: Retrain Cashier to work more efficiently.
Risk: School may not comply with training.
Oversight: Volunteer monitor would have to be onsite daily to enforce compliance; ongoing training given by me.

Improvement Strategy #5: Redirect Mom volunteers to be more hands on.
Risk: A mom telling another mom how to volunteer… never goes well.
Oversight: Ongoing lunch volunteer training. Gosh, who's going to do that? Me!

Improvement Strategy #6: My son no longer eats hot lunch.
Risk: None.
Oversight: Lunch needs to be prepared daily at home.

Improvement Strategy #7: My son continues to eat hot lunch and is responsible for shutting up and eating.
Risk: My son might not have as much fun during lunch.
Oversight: Routinely remind him that whether or not he eats is a direct result of his own behavior choices.

Final Strategy

Objectives (listed in order of importance from Step 2)	Strat. #1 Clean School	Strat. #2 Over-crowd	Strat. #3 Re-design Flow	Strat. #4 Cash Train-ing	Strat. #5 Mom Volun-teers	Strat. #6 No more hot lunch	Strat. #7 My son shuts up and eats WINNER
Get nutrition	No	Maybe	Maybe	No	No	Yes	Yes
Focus for day	No	Maybe	Maybe	Maybe	Maybe	Maybe	Yes
Participate in Recess/Socialize	No	Maybe	Maybe	Maybe	No	Yes	Yes
Enjoy Lunch	Yes	Maybe	Maybe	No	Maybe	No (He really likes hot lunch)	No (He really likes fun.)

Phase #3 - Action

Tools...

The improvement which best met my objectives was Strategy #7, "My son shuts up and eats!" In order to implement this strategy, we needed a little tool called "coaching." The child was placed firmly in a chair and listened to the following instruction: "Stop talking and goofing off during lunch and focus on eating!" A simple strategy and oversight plan with little effort required to keep the result going! A second tool utilized was consequences. Remember, earlier I confessed that I am boundary oriented. Part of what I count on here is that hunger would be an amazing behavior modifier (children rarely starve themselves)!

Phase #4 - Oversight

Measuring Success...

The reports of starvation stopped and there were no reports of an inability to focus. Both of these results were exactly what we wanted. Our objectives were met making the process improvement project a success.

Oversight...

Again, the ongoing support required was minimal. My son needed to be occasionally reminded of his responsibility. Simple. Simple. Simple.

PROBLEM EASED!

(You might wonder why it is not ERASED. Well the reports of starvation stopped. That doesn't mean that there weren't days where my son disregarded instruction and goofed off. We would need proof that it never happened again to say it was ERASED, and that just doesn't seem likely in third grade.)

INTENDED OUTCOME – SUCCESSFUL

(We set out to improve the way the lunch time was being used. We did what we intended, but did not make predictions of any increase in bites or time spent eating. This problem didn't warrant that kind of granularity.)

Case Study C: Distractions

Observations..

Photo: Dolgachov

A Marketing Department is being flooded with distracting phone calls from all over the company. The phone calls could be everything from donation questions, to marketing material needs, to photo requests, to job openings. Emails came in the same way, copied to everyone so that anyone, or everyone, might be quick to answer.

Stakeholders..
- Marketing Staff
- All other employees
- Customers

We couldn't poll the customers, but we could talk with the employees that were the biggest offenders. They confirmed, "Yes, we do bother you for everything because it's easy. Someone will help us out quickly!"

Problem Statement..
Remember: don't overcomplicate the problem statement. The problem statement is simple: Marketing staff is being distracted by inquiry calls and emails not related to their job.

Symptoms/Objectives..
What are the symptoms of the marketing staff being distracted? What are the objectives we are trying to achieve?

Symptom	Objective	Rank
Missed deadlines (because we are spending time on things that aren't ours)	Deadlines are met	1
Overtime (because during the day I am pulled away to help on things I don't own)	Work gets done during business hours	2
Bad morale (team is frustrated)	Improved morale	4
Low Customer Satisfaction (when a customer reaches me and I am not the right person they are upset)	Improved customer experience	3

Phase #2 - Plan

Resources..

- People: How many people are available to help me improve the situation?
    - Marketing Department Staff
- Money: How much money is available to help me improve the situation?
    - None – Are you seeing a trend here?
- Time: How much time do we have to improve the situation?
    - 60 days

Exclusions/Limitations...

We will not... be addressing this problem for the entire company
We will not... leverage any IT resources
We will not... leverage any company database software solutions

Improvement Strategies/Risks/Oversight.....................................

Improvement Strategy #1: Circulate an organizational chart.
Risk: Nobody would look at it, and an organization chart does not have the granularity of detail one might need in order to know who to contact.
Oversight: It would need to be updated when there is a change and recirculated routinely. All callers/emailers would need to be reminded of the organizational chart.

Improvement Strategy #2: Staff meeting introductions for every department.
Risk: Employees might be out that day; there are a lot of departments and this would take a lot of time, possibly even more time than taking the phone calls themselves.
Oversight: Meetings would have to be ongoing and updated information shared routinely.

Improvement Strategy #3: Don't respond to emails and calls that are phishing for a response from marketing unless it's the employee's direct responsibility.
Risk: Issues are delayed in getting addressed. It will be easier to just answer the email.
Oversight: Provide a tool that all employees can access to easily understand who the proper contact is; have discipline internally to not respond to requests that don't belong to this department or the employee, personally.

Improvement Strategy #4: Take responsibility for the calls and appoint a marketing person to field all calls/emails.
Risk: Additional responsibility on a single person could be overwhelming.
Oversight: Amend job description and make certain someone is available during PTO, so these calls are always handled.

Final Strategy

Objectives (listed in order of importance from Step 2)	Strategy #1 Org Chart	Strategy #2 Dept. Meetings	Strategy #3 Don't Respond WINNER	Strategy #4 Appoint Contact
Meet Deadlines	No	No	Yes	Yes
During Business Hours	No	No	Yes	Maybe
Improved Morale	No	Maybe	Yes	No (we have no money to compensate for the extra duties)
Improved Customer Satisfaction	No	Maybe	Maybe	No

Phase #3 - Action

We may not be able to meet all of our objectives, but when we can meet the majority of them it is still a successful process improvement. In this case, the team found Strategy #3 to be the best course of action, don't respond. If the team stopped responding to blast emails, calls, and voice mails that don't belong to them, they would have more time to get their own work done. Over time, the rest of the organization would catch on.

Tools

Two members of the team volunteered to create a departmental organization chart in PowerPoint. (Although no money was allocated to solve this problem, human resources were permitted. Don't kid yourself, time is money.)

The chart included a "tree" like feature that allowed the user to click on a series of buttons which directed them to the right person in the department. The entire department was involved in testing the tool before it was disbursed to the rest of the employees, and they were trained on how to respond to callers and emailers by directing them to the tool 100% of the time.

Phase #4 - Oversight

Measuring Success..
Success? Did we achieve it? The first couple of weeks looked promising, but ultimately the objectives were not met. The project was not successful.

Oversight...
The difficult part of this improvement strategy was the oversight. Forcing people to change their behavior is a time-consuming endeavor, and it can also carry with it a great deal of frustration. This strategy required that every person in the Marketing Department be willing to take an oath to handle calls by stating, "I am sorry, that is not my area of expertise. I will send you a link to the tool that will allow you to identify the right person." If everyone is on board, change of behavior could actually happen. However, if just one person fails to follow the oversight protocol, the time and effort put into creating the tool is a waste. Risky!

Within a month after implementation, many of the employees within the Department were back to fielding multiple calls that didn't belong to them. The strategy was good, the tool was amazing (using software readily available); however, without the ability to control each employee's personal response, or a consequence/reward system to ensure compliance, it fell flat. This is why sometimes it is better to go with a strategy that addresses fewer objectives, but requires a level of oversight that is more manageable. An unmanaged oversight plan can make the entire process a waste of time and might be seen as a failure, when in actuality, the process improvement was sound, but the oversight was unmanageable under the circumstances.

PROBLEM NOT EASED
INTENDED OUTCOME – UNSUCCESSFUL
(The result was intended rather than calculated because we wanted to improve the way time was being spent, but had no way to predict the number of minutes that might be recovered for each employee if successful. To add further insult, no further interest was shown in solving the problem. It was simply dropped, resulting in all the time spent being a loss.)

Case Study D: Overtime Overload

Photo: Imilian

There was a budgeting concern! A single employee is booking weekly overtime hours in the double digits. Her claim was that the custom and last-minute nature of her job required unplanned overtime.

The department in question served an educational need. The company had internal trainers that hosted multiple education courses every week throughout the country, offering continuing education ("CE") credit. Name badges, certificates, meeting handouts and notes needed to be printed on the office copying equipment and sent to the course location prior to the event. Additionally, the venue needed to be reserved and food needed to be provided. In essence, each course was a separate, yet similar, event.

Stakeholders..

- Education Staff and Manager
- Educators
- Onsite Sales Representatives
- Fulfillment Personnel
- Hotel/Venue Staff
- Attendees

Observations..

It seemed logical that the most insight we might be able to gain was from the employee actually doing the job. This stakeholder would carry the greatest portion of the weight. During a 4 hour investigation of the job being completed, here is what was discovered:

- The long-time employee was working as fast as she possibly could, given the tools she had access to and her professional skill level.
- Excel was the tool used to manage registrations, name badges, certificates, etc.
- Records had to be kept for 7 years. This was a regulated requirement connected to CE credits. Each course had its own folder on the computer. If a person called for a copy of a certificate, and they couldn't remember which course they attended, which was most of them, hundreds of files would need to be opened and manually reviewed in order to find the attendee to duplicate the certificate.

- The employee was months, if not years, behind in reporting the attendees to the accreditation authority.
- The number of pages printed for each course was time consuming, not to mention the cost associated with shipping.
- Items returned for processing were often times unprofessional; one came back with the sign in sheet on a yellow legal pad.
- Each course was handled as a brand new request, with no standard operating procedures in place to guide the process.

Problem Statement..

Without imposing solutions, the problem statement became, "Education staff is unable to meet education requirements within normal business hours." Based on observations, the solution might seem evident. Don't be fooled! Keep going through the steps.

Symptoms/Objectives...

What are the symptoms being experienced by our Stakeholders? What objectives do we hope to achieve?

Once we spoke with the stakeholders we uncovered a number of symptoms that went far beyond the "overtime." In this step, the overtime did not rank as the top priority objective.

Symptom	Objective	Rank
Overtime paid weekly (unbudgeted)	Work gets done during business hours	4
Inability to provide documentation required by regulatory agencies	Ability to track 7 years of data quickly and efficiently (legal requirement)	1
Inconsistent presence onsite at training sessions	Consistent, professional experience for staff and attendees regardless of the location	2
Out of control costs related to copying and shipping	Streamline print/ship process	5
Unable to cross train	Documented process that can be followed by multiple employees	3

Phase #2 - Plan

Resources..

- People: How many people are available to help me improve the situation?
  - Manager
  - 2 additional staff members

- Money: How much money is available to help me improve the situation?
  - None (Is there ever any money for process improvement?)
- Time: How much time do we have to improve the situation?
  - Undetermined

Exclusions/Limitations...

Before moving on with this problem, it was important to get a handle on the exclusions. You see, the employee had been with the company for 25 years. She was well liked. However, if we weren't willing to insist on the use of the new process we may build, little could be done to impact the problem. We needed to know this up front. After speaking with the managing authority, it was determined that the limitations would be:

We will not... be locked into old processes
We will not... be bound to current staff selections
We will not... leverage any IT resources
We will not... leverage any company database software solutions

You might ask why IT and company databases were not leveraged. In this company, leveraging these resources and tools meant a whole new level of approvals and putting this initiative in a pipeline over 12 months out. This would also elevate the IT team to a higher Stakeholder level, putting them in a position to speak loudly into a situation they knew nothing about, and had no impact their department. It wasn't worth it.

Improvement Strategies/Risks/Oversight...

Improvement Strategy #1: Document the current process.
Risk: Then we could have two employees who follow a bad process.
Oversight: Make sure the documentation evolves if the process changes.

Improvement Strategy #2: Create a standardized process for education requests and support.
Risk: Building and training could take time. Skillset may not be there.
Oversight: Requirement to learn and follow the new process from top down.

Improvement Strategy #3: Convert printed resources to digital resources.
Risk: Attendees won't like not having printed material; printing their own will result in printing many pages.
Oversight: Create a system where the digital files are updated routinely as determined by the trainers.

Improvement Strategy #4: Provide computer training to current employee.
Risk: She still might not get it. The tools she is currently using may not be the right tools. Refining skills on the wrong tools is a risk.
Oversight: Once she had the education, continual management oversight will be required to ensure the new skills are utilized in a way to impact the problem.

Objectives (listed in order of importance from Step 2)	Strategy #1 Document Current Process	Strategy #2 Create Standardized Process	Strategy #3 Print to Digital Conversion	Strategy #4 Computer Training
Ability to efficiently track 7 years of education data	No	Yes **WINNER**	No	No
Consistent Experience for staff and attendees	No	Yes	No	No
Documented process for cross training	Yes	Yes	No	No
Work gets accomplished in normal work day	No	Maybe	Yes	No
Streamline costs related to attendee documents	No	No	Yes	No

Phase #3 - Action

In this case, improvement strategy #2, "Create a Standardized Process," was selected and the choice was to utilize the Process Improvement Specialist on staff (me) to make it happen. Note! Improvement strategy #2 does not meet all the objectives. Sometimes, problems are complex and the objectives need to be addressed in phases.

Tools...

This strategy required several tools, including an online request form, and an Access database that imported all attendee information and was able to then print Sign-in sheets, name badges, and certificates, with a click of a button. The onsite staff representative received a binder 2-3 days prior to the event which included everything they needed to present a professional and consistent event.

The venues received an RFP and were required to provide consistent rooms, equipment, and lunch, so that all events were similar in look and feel. The documentation was contained within the database, and attendees could be found by their name, contact information, course attended, year attended, location, etc. The details could be located in seconds and the replacement certificate could be printed instantly, meeting the legal and contractual requirements. (5 years of prior data kept in Excel had to be converted.)

Phase #4 - Oversight

Measuring Success...
Achieving success is more than just a feeling. In this situation, when we reviewed all of the objectives, we were able to say we met all of the intended objectives, and even the unintended objectives – over time! If it takes time to implement the process, be patient about measuring success until the implementation is complete and the process has time to be utilized.

Oversight...
It took close to 6 months to develop all of the necessary components, and about a year to get everyone moving in a new direction. There were many accusations of "inflexibility" as employees tried to do things the old way. Management's support, and a strong personality, were required to avoid the boomerang effect back into bad habits.

The employee who had been with the company for 25 years retired. After she left, overtime was no longer required. An additional employee was not necessary and the objective we originally weren't sure if we would be able to meet, "Work gets accomplished in normal work day," went from a "Maybe" to a "Yes." We like it when that happens!

Once our anticipated outcomes were met and controlled over about a two year time frame, it was time to go back to the objective we did not achieve with the first improvement strategy. Phase II addressed streamlining costs related to attendee documents or "going green." All documents were made digital and attendees were alerted to download and print documents prior to their event. Oh, Yes! Even though things were going well, and progress was happening, there was still push back.

You might think we are done! During the improvements, it was revealed that a more automated approach to attendee communication would be the icing on the cake! Phase III became converting the attendee communication from a manual process in Outlook, to a semi-automated process through an email client. This is a great example of a situation that called for consecutive improvement strategies. We couldn't meet all of the objectives at once. However, attacking the first improvement made the second and third possible.

The system has been used for eight years and counting with a budget line item of zero dollars.

PROBLEM EASED!
INTENDED OUTCOME – SUCCESSFUL
(The improvement intended to increase efficiency, and in doing so, also decreased resource expenses and provided tangible tools. Because we did not go into this project with specifics around dollars or time saved, we cannot call it a calculated result. However, it turned out to be an intended outcome that did more than first expected.)

Case Study E: Contract Catastrophe

Photo: Pavel

A Fortune 500 Company which provided state-of-the art services to the healthcare industry had a problem. They contracted with many states to provide a complex service. Some contracts had over 50 deliverables, many of which came with cash penalties if not met.

One of the states scheduled their annual review, and after detailing all of the missed contract deliverables, were paid millions in penalties… about $16 million to be more specific. Houston! We have a problem! But, which problem did we have? Is it the contract department, the sales department, or the product department at fault? If we just went forward with, "Our salespeople aren't managing their contracts," how would that sit with our sales department, who definitely represent stakeholders? Do you think they might have some insight to offer?

Stakeholders...
- Sales Staff
- Product Management Staff
- Contracting
- Customers

Now is a good time to point out that this issue was unique in that the individual that identified the problem and championed the improvement was upper management. She not only had the expertise and insight, but she had the **authority**. She carved out the necessary time to pull both the sales and product management teams together to understand the conflicting and converging requirements. When you get to work with a stakeholder of this caliber, enjoy it, because it is not a common occurrence.

Observations..
Some investigation was in order. After talking with stakeholders, we found that this problem had existed for years. At least two attempts had been made to solve the problem, unsuccessfully. Over time, and with turnover of staff, it had been accepted that these contracts would just incur some kind of penalty… it was the company's definition of normal in the absence of a total solution.

This is a good time to ask, "Why didn't the other solutions work?" Let's go back to the section on "Change" and how much it hurts. If you are implementing a new process that is going to require an employee to learn a new system which might require more time than just doing nothing... what is their incentive? Are they getting paid more? Probably not. Are they getting a promotion with the perceived new responsibilities? Probably not. So why on earth would they comply? The only reason any employee begins to comply is because they feel they have no choice but to comply, and that message needs to come from the top. There needs to be someone in a position of authority that will draw a hard line and force compliance. The employee will continue to comply, willingly, once they start seeing the personal benefit to their time management or professional reputation. I mean, let's face it! Nobody wants to be the guy managing the contract that just dinged the company $16 Million in penalties! Right?

Maybe the problem isn't the people, but the process.

Problem Statement..
The problem statement was "Contract terms are not being managed in a manner which avoids penalty."

Notice that this problem statement does not point the finger at a particular person or department as being at fault. That is very important at this point because we don't know the root cause. It also does not lead us to a solution, because we don't know that yet either.

Symptoms/Objectives..
What are the symptoms related to not meeting contract deliverables? What do we hope to achieve?

Symptom	Objective	Rank
Large Monetary Penalties	Limit Monetary Penalties	1
Contract Deliverables not Met	Contract Deliverables Met	2
Customer Satisfaction Low	Increased Customer Satisfaction	4
Disconnect between Sales and Product Management	Collaboration between Sales and Product Management	6
Inability to hand off contract management when there is turnover	Contract management documented for easy transition to new employees	5
Inability to predict a problem with meeting contract deliverables in time to course correct	Insight into contract issues in time to course correct	3

Resources...

In this case, the insight into the problem and the process improvement idea was identified by a fairly new employee in upper management. She was able to see the problem quickly, where long-time employees had become blind. Because there were millions of dollars on the line, only a "velvet hammer" was needed. However, she was completely prepared to use the "hammer" if necessary.

- People: How many people are available to help me improve the situation?
    - Manager
    - Sales Staff
    - Product Management Staff
- Money: How much money is available to help me improve the situation?
    - None (Not even a Fortune 500 company providing state-of-the-art solutions across the world will put any money toward this improvement...very frustrating!)
- Time: How much time do we have to improve the situation?
    - 6 months

Exclusions/Limitations...

This is a big company! Without exclusions there are many departments which will want to have input on this project.

We will not... be able to utilize any of the corporate systems or databases
We will not... look to solve contract issues outside this department
We will not... leverage any IT resources (their pipeline was overflowing)

Improvement Strategies/Risks/Oversight.....................................

Improvement Strategy #1: Ask each sales manager to develop, document, and implement their own contract management process.
Risk: Inconsistent and insufficient oversight. Kind of like grading your own math paper.
Oversight: Self-managed; Each manager would be responsible for ensuring they follow their own plan.

Improvement Strategy #2: Hire a contract manager to monitor contracts for compliance.
Risk: Complication building accountability and ownership; a lot to learn and understand. No money for new hire.
Oversight: Meetings between employees/contract compliance manager monthly to understand and report status.

Improvement Strategy #3: Implement a monetary penalty to sales staff if their contract incurs a penalty.
Risk: Nobody would want the job. Turnover would be critical to the ability to manage deliverables, which could actually increase penalties.
Oversight: Continual employment contracting, hiring and training.

Improvement Strategy #4: Build tool to manage contract deliverables
Risk: Lack of cooperation
Oversight: Report must be submitted monthly and all reports combined to be reviewed at the upper management level. Compliance must be non-negotiable.

Final Strategy..

Objectives (listed in order of importance from Step 2)	Strategy #1 Individual Process	Strategy #2 Hire Contract Manager	Strategy #3 Monetary Penalty to Sales	Strategy #4 Create a tool – Require everyone to use it.
Limit monetary penalties	Maybe	Yes	Maybe	**WINNER** Yes
Contract deliverables met	Maybe	Yes	No	Yes
Insight to problems in time to course correct	No	Yes	No	Yes
Increased customer satisfaction	Maybe	Yes	No	Yes
Documented for ease of transition	No	No	No	Yes
Collaboration between sales and product management	No	No	No	Yes

Phase #3 - Action

We've got two strategies with good scores. Strategy #2, "Hire a Contract Manager," does not meet all of our objectives, but it could be implemented much more quickly, with less of an impact on the existing staff.

Ooops!! Go back to resources! There is no money! There is no salary for a contract administrator to solve this problem. In spite of the sense it would make, the resources don't support this improvement strategy. You might ask "Why are we including this strategy in the first place?" With all the information you have now, would it be possible to go back to management and make a more solid case for investing in the improvement? Well, it couldn't hurt! In this case, the answer was still no money. But we tried!

Strategy #4 it is, "Create a Contract Management Tool and Make Everyone Use it!"

Tools..

Each contract would have its own scorecard, half updated by the sales staff member, and half updated by the product manager. The scorecard would allow both departments to monitor the contract deliverables and the product on a monthly basis, with a "red-yellow-green" stoplight report which indicated the need for increased attention in real time.

Once the tool was finalized, with the gold seal of approval from the stakeholders, the training began. A series of workshops assisted the nationwide sales staff in converting the contract deliverables into the scorecard items, and then several months of individual tutoring was made available.

Phase #4 - Oversight

Measure Success..

This strategy was recognized as the "Process Improvement of the Year." The tool was being used long after the manager who conceptualized the idea and the process/tool creator and Oversight Manager moved on from the company. The reason it was utilized beyond the life of those that created it is because the improvement was sound for the company, not just a pet project for the individual attempting to improve the process. Once the stakeholders started to reap the benefits of objectives achieved, the motivation to continue use was self-sustaining.

Oversight...

This project took over a year to implement. Each month it was expected that the scorecards would be updated and forwarded to management for review. Hands-on oversight was required to keep the improvement working. Each month there were some that lagged in meeting their deadlines, and a strong resolve to enforce the requirement to submit was routine. Without a strong and consistent oversight plan, and unwavering support from upper management, this process would have surely failed within 90 days, just like the two prior attempts.

There was no additional monetary cost for the tool. It was simply an excel spreadsheet, elaborately coded, but an excel spreadsheet nonetheless. You do the math. $16M in penalties on one contract averted with a tool the company already owned. Not every process improvement strategy needs to cost a fortune. Sometimes talking with stakeholders can reveal unique skills that can offer support never before available.

PROBLEM EASED!
INTENDED OUTCOME – SUCCESSFUL
(Even though we know the implementation of this improvement strategy saved money, AND LOTS OF IT, we couldn't predict how much or what components of the project would be responsible for what percentage of the savings. The project began as an efficiency project that common sense and logic dictated would result in savings. That is why it is an intended outcome rather than a calculated outcome.

CHAPTER 6
Cooperation & Willingness!
It all comes back to the Horse and the Water

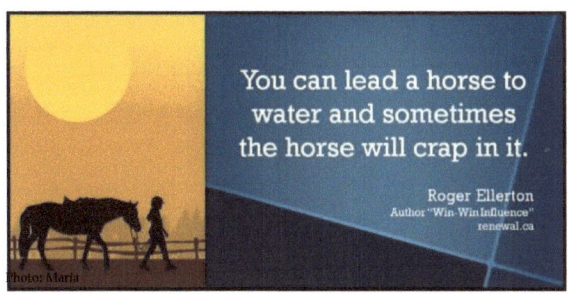

You can lead a horse to water and sometimes the horse will crap in it.

Roger Ellerton
Author "Win-Win Influence"
renewal.ca

Remember David, King of the Foyer? That situation was a complete success. I could not have asked for a better outcome. However, the credit does not go completely to me. Okay, I will take a good portion, but without David's cooperation and willingness to comply, it would not have mattered how sound my mentoring, or how beautiful my forms. David could have refused to cooperate. He could have embraced his stress and held onto his beliefs and kept right on doing what he was doing. He would have been fired, and another solution would have been implemented (a much more expensive, time consuming, and risky solution with no guarantee of a better outcome).

You see, as a person who is implementing a process improvement, your biggest hurdle is not the problem statement or the selection of an improvement strategy, it's the people. If the people are not willing or cooperative, you are dead in the water... or shall we say, "crapped on" in the water!

There is a difference between cooperation and willingness. We love to have both, but that doesn't always happen.

Cooperative implies that the person will do what they are told without going out of their way to sabotage the process. Cooperation does not require excitement or comradery over an issue.

Willingness implies that there is buy in. The person has at some level agreed with the theories and ideas, and supports the endeavors necessary to make the improvement. Willingness brings with it a sense of approval, and creates a much lighter attitude; it also almost always comes hand in hand with cooperation. Cooperation is what we expect from an employee, willingness is what we aspire to achieve with that employee, through the process.

What will you achieve if you can't get cooperation and willingness? Absolutely nothing! Which takes us full circle to our stakeholders and the importance to involve them, engage them, and listen to them. Stakeholder cooperation and/or willingness will be critical to your success.

If your stakeholders become uncooperative during a project, it is usually because they no longer see what's in it for them. There are a couple of ways you can address the potentially harmful attitudes:

1. Remind Them!
    Constantly remind them of what's in it for them. Make sure you are reviewing your symptoms and objectives often, so that they don't forget why they are involved in this project.

2. Communicate With Them!
    A stakeholder that is removed from the progress and success of the project will naturally become disengaged. If a project lasts a long time, they can also get bored. Increase your communication. Now, I don't mean send a weekly email telling them what you have done, and how you see things. I don't mean that you should hold another meeting to go over what you still need. Be careful about communication, you don't want your stakeholders to feel like they are being "talked to" rather than "talked with." This will only create more distance.

    Instead, invite your stakeholders to contribute to the communication. What is their status? What do they need? What were their successes? Plan a lunch, or a retreat, or a team building event. A little fun can go a long way to keeping your team engaged.

3. Separate Them!
    Attitudes can be contagious, good or bad. If you start to sense that your stakeholder team is no longer on your side, there can be a benefit to sitting down with each one, separate from the rest, and getting the scoop. This may help you identify if there is a single stakeholder that is "spoiling the pot."

I wish I could say, "Don't let stakeholders stand in your way!" But I can't. If your improvement project impacts these individuals, you simply can't disregard them, because you can't do it without them. Instead, if stakeholders are standing in your way, find out why! Keeping them engaged is part of the project leader's responsibility if you want your improvement to be successful.

What if you can't gain cooperation or willingness?

Sometimes people will not be converted. Maybe it's pride, arrogance, laziness, or self-serving attitudes. Many times we may never know exactly what keeps someone from getting on board. If it's one person on a team of ten that is uncooperative, we can use the ideas shared previously and a number of conflict resolution and negotiation tactics to deal with the person. What if the uncooperative attitude expands to others? Regardless of the reason for the barrier, if your stakeholder team becomes uncooperative and unwilling to participate, there will come a time when you have to waive the white flag and surrender. At some point, you will have to allow the group, team, or individual to operate as they wish, even if that means they operate with dysfunction or inefficiencies – even if they choose broken. You have to let it go. This is an especially tough thing to do for those looking to make things better, and is typically not quick to happen.

I was approached by an organization who wanted to hire an Executive Director. I communicated my services clearly and detailed the level of expertise that I brought to the table. I was also very clear that if they were looking for an hourly task master, I was not their gal. I was very certain that my brutal honesty in the interview process ensured I would not be hired. Wrong! They hired me and so it began; from day one there was an unwillingness to advance or innovate.

Three and a half years later, the struggle had not lessened. It actually got worse as the board became a revolving door, assigning responsibility and authority to those that knew nothing about the organization or what they had said they wanted. It became all too clear that this organization wanted to remain exactly as it used to be. The organization they said they wanted to become, was no longer the goal, and any progress that had been made could not sustain the constant battle to go back to the way things used to be.

How long do you fight it? How long to try to facilitate improvement? It will look different for every situation. After three and a half years I decided it was time to let this group continue on their path without me, for the sake of us both. By letting go of the organization, I was free to direct my energy toward more positive interactions, and they were free to make their own decisions. For the first time in three and half years, we had a win-win!

It is a common occurrence that people will ask for things they really don't want. Our goal is to vet this during our "insight" phase, but sometimes it is buried deep in culture, and we won't see it until later in the process. I see it a lot in member based organizations. Members will ask for more education, and when you provide it, nobody will come. Members will ask for more networking, and when you plan it, numbers remain low. In the case of the organization once understood they needed to change, they just didn't want to have to actually have to change anything to get there. That just simply won't work!

CHAPTER 7
Start Small and Practice!

"An ounce of practice is generally worth more than a ton of theory."
— Ernst F. Schumacher

An entire generation of kids thought they knew how to play the guitar because they excelled at Guitar Hero®. When my child was on his way to his first snowboarding excursion, he was confident he was going to sail down the slopes. His confidence was based solely on the fact that he was pretty good at SSX Tricky®, a snowboarding video game. Yep, regardless of the hours he spent playing that game, he failed to master even the most elementary slope. He spent some quality time on his rear end because he never did the hard work – he never practiced the real deal!

Now that you have the process improvement theory, it is imperative to practice, in real life. Don't start with the high profile, high risk problems. For someone who aspires to be a marathon runner, my suggestion is practice running around the block before taking on the mile… and the mile before the 5K.

I promised you it was simple, and I think I have kept that promise.
Look at your pain points and determine which ones you can actually impact.

- Insight!
  Engage your stakeholders, make observations, develop a problem statement, and identify and rank your symptoms and objectives.
- Plan!
  Move forward by understanding your resources, limitations and exclusions. List all the improvement strategies and then weigh them against your desired objectives to choose the best strategy for the problem.
- Action!
  Communicate your expectations and guidelines and give your stakeholders a job as part of your strategy. Decide which tools will be required for your strategy; build them if you have to.
- Oversight!
  Is your strategy improving your situation? If so, keep watching and listening, additional opportunities may be revealed. If not, be prepared to tweak your strategy.

Take a look around your personal environment and identify something simple. Develop a problem statement around the copier always being out of ink, the trash never being emptied, or the distraction of a chatty cubicle neighbor. Walk through the steps to identify and implement a process improvement project. Don't take shortcuts, and don't skip steps. Practice is only a good thing if you are practicing right!

Take on and improve one issue a month until you are comfortable with the process. Your comfort level will allow you to graduate to more difficult problems with confidence that improvement is possible and it can change your situation for the better.

Go forth and enjoy the process because the benefit to you is just one improvement away!

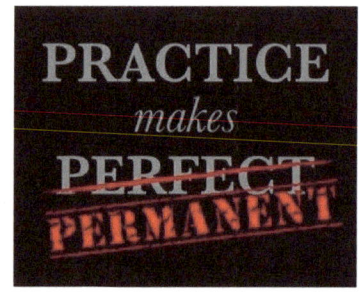

Pumpkin Bars

Critical to Consume During the "Insight" Phase of Your Next Process Improvement Project

Ingredients

- 4 Eggs
- 2 C Sugar
- 1 ½ C Canola or Vegetable Oil
- 1 Can Pumpkin (Large)
- 3 Tsp Baking Soda
- 1 Tsp Salt
- 2 Tsp Cinnamon
- 2 ½ C Flour
- (For gluten free, use 2 ¼ Cups of Pillsbury Gluten Free Flour with Xantham Gum instead of regular flour. Your guests will never even know ☺!)
- You will need a Jelly Roll Pan (not a cake pan) and a Hand or Standing Mixer

Plan to stand at the mixer. Mix in order given, making certain that each ingredient is added slowly and fully incorporated before the next one is added. (Remember, if you add the ingredients in a different order, it doesn't turn out the same!)

Pour in jelly roll pan and bake for 25-30 minutes at 350 degrees. (Different ovens require different times, the key is not over-baking. I check with a toothpick at about 18 minutes, and keep checking about every 2 or 3 minutes after. You want to pull it out as soon as the toothpick comes out with crumbles – not completely clean.)

Once removed from the oven, use wax paper or parchment paper to put pressure on the cake making it level on top. You may have to push down a bit, and that's ok. Allow to cool completely.

Frosting

- 3 to 5 C Powdered Sugar
- 3 - 8 oz Cream Cheese
- 2 Sticks of Butter
- 3 Tsp Vanilla

Cream butter and cream cheese together. I beat them for a long time (5min.) Add vanilla. Add sugar, one cup at a time, to your liking. I start taste testing at 3 Cups of sugar added and usually don't go much beyond that, because I don't like the frosting sweet, sweet.

Spread on completely cooled bars, and refrigerate. These are actually better if you let them sit for a day.

Jodi began her career in the corporate world over thirty years ago. From the obscure "mom and pop" to the Fortune 500 companies, Jodi has held a variety of different responsibilities and has seen more opportunities for process improvement than she cares to count. Through her desire to become an expert in all things Microsoft, combined with her unique ability to see improvement opportunities all around, she quickly became the "go to" person when problems needed to be solved.

In 2010, Jodi started her own business managing professional trade associations. She puts her skills to use guiding and directing Boards of non-profits to improve the way they deliver value to members. In this environment, she finds opportunities for processes improvement daily!

In addition to her hands-on non-profit clients, Jodi has packaged her experience for businesses looking to develop their employees and empower them to make improvements. She presents for luncheons, keynotes, or detailed workshops to meet the specific needs of corporate and non-profit organizations.

Jodi's 20 years of experience performing on stage, and her anecdotal style, enables her to communicate with ease, humor, and relatable stories, allowing groups of any size to walk away with practical ideas delivered in an entertaining way.

Jodi is a native of Colorado, having grown up in Littleton, and currently resides in Thornton, CO, with her husband, John, of 27 years. They work together in their business, and cite separate offices as a critical component to success.

John and Jodi enjoy their blended family of 5 grown children and 4 grandchildren! They try not to be too happy about being "empty nesters," and have found this season of life energizing!

Schedule Jodi for your next event.
www.jodiholstein.com

www.ingramcontent.com/pod-product-compliance
Lightning Source LLC
Chambersburg PA
CBHW040832180526
45159CB00001B/160